Roger Williams

Prophet of Liberty

OXFORD
PORTRAITS

Roger Williams

Prophet of Liberty

Edwin S. Gaustad

OXFORD
UNIVERSITY PRESS

*To the spiritual heirs of Roger Williams, to those who agree
with him that "having bought truth dear, we must not sell it
cheap, not the least grain of it for the whole world."*

OXFORD
UNIVERSITY PRESS

Oxford   New York
Athens Auckland Bangkok Bogotá Buenos Aires Calcutta
Cape Town Chennai Dar es Salaam Delhi Florence Hong Kong Istanbul
Karachi Kuala Lumpur Madrid Melbourne Mexico City Mumbai
Nairobi Paris São Paulo Singapore Taipei Tokyo Toronto Warsaw
and associated companies in
Berlin   Ibadan

Copyright © 2001 by Edwin S. Gaustad
Published by Oxford University Press, Inc.
198 Madison Avenue, New York, New York 10016
www.oup.com

Oxford is a registered trademark of Oxford University Press

Design: Greg Wozney
Layout: Alexis Siroc
Picture research: Amla Sanghvi

Library of Congress Cataloging-in-Publication Data
Gaustad, Edwin S. (Edwin Scott)
Roger Williams: prophet of liberty / Edwin S. Gaustad.
p. cm. — (Oxford portraits)
Includes bibliographical references and index.
ISBN 0-19-513000-6
1. Williams, Roger, 1604?–1683—Juvenile literature. 2. Puritans—Rhode Island
—Biography—Juvenile literature. 3. Baptists—Rhode Island—Biography—
Juvenile literature. 4. Separatists—Rhode Island—Biography—Juvenile literature.
5. Pioneers—Rhode Island—Biography—Juvenile literature. 6. Freedom of religion—Rhode Island—History—17th century—Juvenile literature. 7. Freedom of
religion—United States—History—Juvenile literature. 8. Rhode Island—Church
history—17th century—Juvenile literature. [1. Williams, Roger, 1604?–1683. 2.
Reformers. 3. Puritans. 4. Rhode Island—History—Colonial period, ca.
1600–1775. 5. Freedom of religion.] I. Title. II. Series.

F82.W7 G38 2000
974.5'02'092--dc21
[B]   00-056675

9 8 7 6 5 4 3 2 1

Printed in the United States of America
on acid-free paper

On the cover and frontispiece: Bronze sculpture of Roger Williams at Roger
Williams University in Bristol, Rhode Island.

CONTENTS

PREFACE

At first glance, Roger Williams does not seem like a promising subject for a biography. We do not know when he was born, nor exactly when he died. We do not know what he looked like. We cannot visit his home, for it went up in flames long ago. Although he was a preacher, no sermon of his survives. During his lifetime, not a single monument was erected in his honor and, at his death, no carved stone marked his grave. He was—or so it appeared—a forgotten man.

Slowly, however, the memory of the man has begun to be reclaimed. If he was a person well ahead of his times, the times have gradually caught up. Scattered writings about his life, often hurriedly composed, were in the latter half of the 19th century gathered together in six volumes; in the 20th century a seventh volume was added. Recollections of his contemporaries, both friends and foes—he had more of the latter—required more careful examination. Tiny steps that he took in the 17th century now look, from the perspective of some 300 years later, like giant strides.

Williams wrote much about the Native Americans, a great deal about the nature of civil government, but most about the proper relationship between things of the spirit and matters of the sword. We still puzzle over exactly where to draw the line between the authority of the state and the freedom of the soul. We still agonize over the folly of religious persecution, both in America and abroad. And we still worry about the limits of liberty as these relate to calls for responsibility. If any such matters seem urgent in the opening years of the 21st century, then Roger Williams needs to be a remembered rather than a forgotten man. His life and his words command our attention.

This 1577 engraving symbolizes the growing sea power of England in the second half of the 16th century. Queen Elizabeth is enthroned at the upper right. The banners in Greek speak to England's increasing military might and to Elizabeth's promotion of Christianity.

THE RESTLESS PURITAN

Religious turbulence and turmoil plagued England in the 17th century, as they had in the 16th. In the 16th century, England, under the prompting of King Henry VIII (1509–47), had broken with the pope and the Roman Catholic Church. But how "Protestant" this made the newly created Church of England was a much-debated question. Then, in her five-year reign beginning in 1553, Queen Mary I tried unsuccessfully to bring England back into the fold of the Roman church. This created great confusion in both domestic and foreign policy, even as it made suspicions and fears of "Catholic plots" an enduring feature of subsequent English life.

In 1558 Queen Elizabeth I ascended to the throne of England. Her reign, unlike that of her two predecessors, would be a long one: 45 years, ending only with her death in 1603. Historians speak of this period as the "Elizabethan settlement," because many aspects of English life and literature (this was the age of Shakespeare) took on their lasting character then. Religious unrest continued, however, especially among believers who argued that the national Church of England, or Anglican Church, had not become

Protestant enough. These fervent Christians thought that England—like Holland and Scotland—should more faithfully follow the theologian John Calvin, then living and writing in Geneva, Switzerland. Many other Protestants had fled during the years that Queen Mary I tried to turn England again toward the Roman Catholic Church. In Geneva these refugees sat at the feet of Calvin for their instruction. A generation before Calvin, a German professor and theologian, Martin Luther, launched the Protestant Reformation by rejecting much traditional theology and practice, relying only on the Holy Scriptures. Now Calvin, as a second generation reformer, worked at presenting a more detailed and systematic defence of the Protestant movement.

Elizabeth, however, was not fully persuaded to become a Calvinist. Like her father, King Henry VIII, she steered a middle path between Roman Catholicism on the one hand and an aggressive Calvinism on the other. When she died in 1603, the Tudor dynasty came to an end. To begin a new royal family, James I of Scotland ascended to the English throne in 1603—the first of the Stuart line of England's monarchs. This shift from Tudor kings and queens to Stuart sovereigns hinted of major changes to come. Also, Roger Williams, probably born in this same year, would eventually do more than hint of momentous changes that needed to be made in both politics and religion.

Born in London, Roger Williams grew to manhood during the reign of James I, who ruled until 1625. When James died, Williams would have been about 22 years of age, having begun his college education at Cambridge University, some 50 miles north of London. At Cambridge (one of England's two ancient universities), Williams studied to be a minister in the Church of England. He fell in with other students who shared the passion that this great church should turn away from any lingering traces of Catholicism in order to embrace a consistent and powerful Protestantism. Those who held these strong views came to be called Puritans:

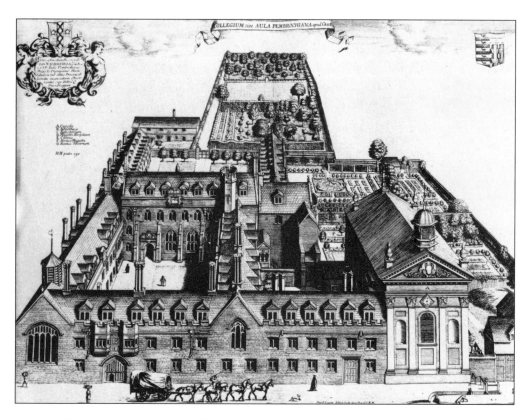

persons determined to cleanse their national church of such lingering elements of Catholic practice as bowing at the name of Jesus and making the sign of the cross at baptism. Puritans also believed, unlike Roman Catholics, that clergy should be allowed to marry and should have sufficient learning to preach a sermon at least every Sunday. Bishops should be pastors, not politicians, and the decision to excommunicate a person (that is, eject him or her from the church) should be a spiritual, not a political, decision.

Because James I had grown up in Calvinist Scotland, many Puritans thought he would be sympathetic to their position. He was not. He believed that the Church of England needed to be his close ally in political as well as in spiritual matters. He did agree, however, to one demand of the Puritans: that a new translation of the Bible into English be provided. By virtue of this concession, James managed to

In 1627, Roger Williams graduated from Pembroke College of Cambridge University in England. Almost all of New England's early Puritan ministers were Cambridge graduates.

associate his name with the most lasting English translation: the King James Version, though, to be sure, he did none of the translating himself. Otherwise, James demanded even stricter conformity to the national church than the English had practiced up to then. This meant that Englishmen and women had to worship in accordance with the prayers and rituals set down in the Book of Common Prayer, the official guide to the church service. Spontaneous prayer and any sort of free-flowing service of worship was not only not allowed; it was illegal. Those who did not conform, identified formally as Nonconformists, fell afoul of England's laws.

To stay in England meant either to conform, at great cost to the Puritans' consciences, or to enter prison, at great cost to their welfare and perhaps even their lives. Some who despaired of ever reforming the bureaucratic Church of England even withdrew from that national body, thereby making themselves targets for arrest and imprisonment. One such group fled to Holland when Roger Williams was still a young boy, and in 1620 emigrated to America aboard the *Mayflower*. This small fellowship, known in American history as the Pilgrims, settled in Plymouth, Massachusetts, where, years later, their history and that of Roger Williams would intersect.

Meanwhile, back in England, the larger body of Puritans still hoped to change the direction of their national church. It was indeed *their* church, their nurturing mother, and they would neither abandon nor forsake it. In the late 1620s, Roger Williams numbered himself among those who hoped for the reformation of all England rather than to move toward a separation and exile from England. But if England proved stubborn and unyielding, as James I had been and King Charles I was now proving to be, then a bold and daring step might be required. Some Puritans came up with an ingenious idea: If they could not persuade the great church at home to change its ways, then perhaps they could—in a faraway corner of land—create what they envisioned as the true church of Christ, which could then become the model for the true Church of England. Far from England's intruding and persecuting bishops, distant from the nation's nosy and arresting sheriffs, the Puritans, taking only the New Testament as their pattern and guide, could fashion a pure, nonpolitical, uncorrupted, noncompromised church.

It *was* bold and daring, so much so as almost to take one's breath away. But gradually, more and more Puritans saw this step as perhaps the only honorable one remaining to them. Not just ministers but lawyers, middle-class farmers, and skilled laborers caught the vision and shared the excitement. Leave England in one sense, but go to England's new lands across the Atlantic, so that they could still be part of their nation and of its church. More than just a part, however—they could be a light, a beacon, an instructor and guide, showing their homeland the path to true Christianity and the meaning of true loyalty. In New England, they would not forsake their nation: they would redeem it.

The Book of Common Prayer, adopted during the reign of Queen Elizabeth, set the prescribed form of worship for all English citizens, whether members of the Church of England or not.

Late in 1629, Roger Williams married Mary Barnard, the daughter of a clergyman. The young couple, Roger about 26 and Mary 20, had hardly adjusted to their new life together when even greater adjustments were required. For Roger and Mary would soon be part of that large Puritan migration from old England to New. Thousands in the 1630s left farms, families, and fortunes behind to create, in and around Boston, a colony of stability and strength sufficient to leave a permanent stamp upon all of America's later history.

At the end of 1630, Roger and Mary Williams journeyed to the port of Bristol, on England's southwest coast. There they and 20 other passengers, boarded the small ship *Lyon* to set out across a treacherous, wintry sea. In less than two months (considered a good crossing in the first half of the 17th century) the *Lyon* dropped anchor, on February 5, 1631, off Nantasket, Massachusetts, a few miles south of Boston. The governor of the newly formed Massachusetts Bay Colony expressed his delight at the arrival of the new colonists, and especially of "Mr. Williams, a godly minister," accompanied by his young wife.

The colony had not gotten off to a great start, for food was scarce, housing primitive, and the winter more severe than any known back in England. Death and disease stalked the tiny colony. Yet new arrivals brought with them fresh supplies and new hope. Within a very few years, the pressing question of survival had been settled. The Massachusetts Bay Colony would not only survive but would eventually flourish. John Winthrop, a lawyer and the governor of the Bay Colony, had earlier spoken of his vision of the colony as a "city on a hill." Slowly, the vision began to take on a measure of reality.

Roger Williams's situation seemed quite promising at first. A new colony eager to receive a "godly minister" into its midst, a land of boundless opportunity and promise, a warm welcome from John Winthrop: all this would certainly have worked in Williams's favor. Roger and Mary soon made their way to Boston, the small settlement that would serve as the center for the Massachusetts Bay Colony. There the young couple found welcome, and even the promise of a secure livelihood. Williams was invited to become the resident minister of the newly organized church in Boston—a Puritan church of the type that would later be called "Congregational," a term emphasizing the point that each local congregation ruled itself without the help (or interference) of bishops or church councils.

At this point, however, Williams made a decision as fateful as the one to step aboard the *Lyon* in Bristol. Despite having no other visible means of support, he decided to turn down the job offer because this Puritan church had not clearly, cleanly separated itself from the Church of England. Boston's Puritans still clung to the idea that they could reform the national church from within, that it was not necessary to separate from or reject that nurturing mother. For Williams this seemed an illogical, and perhaps even hypocritical, compromise. How could one profess loyalty to a church while at the same time being dedicated to changing or reforming that church?

So Roger and Mary struck out for Salem, about 15 miles north of Boston, where a church had been organized along more separatist lines, based on thinking more in keeping with Williams's growing conviction that one must leave the Church of England wholly behind. Because ministers were in short supply in Salem, as in Boston, the Salem church took steps to install Williams in a position of leadership. But the Boston authorities, miffed at Williams's refusal to serve their church and disturbed by his separatist "radicalism," advised Salem to hold off hiring Williams as their pastor. (In Congregationalism, each church remained theoretically independent; at the same time, the town of Salem could hardly afford to ignore or alienate the political powers slowly gathering in Boston.) Salem delayed, and Williams was given no official post in the church. But he still talked, still wrote, and still disturbed those intent on building that "city on a hill."

If Salem was under the thumb of Boston, perhaps, thought Roger and Mary Williams, they would do better moving about 30 miles south of Boston to the Plymouth Colony. These settlers were unmistakably separatists. Having left the Church of England before they went to Holland, they separated long before they boarded the *Mayflower.* In Plymouth the restless Roger Williams might have hoped to

find congenial company and a welcoming home. And from late 1631 to the fall of 1633 this almost seemed to be the case. But then, as the Plymouth governor, William Brewster, reported in his valuable history *Of Plimouth Plantation,* Williams "began to fall into some strange opinions, and from opinion to practice." So Williams, rather abruptly, left the church in Plymouth to return to Salem. Though it is not clear just what his "strange opinions"

This modern replica of the Mayflower, *built in England, is 104 feet long and 25 feet wide. In 1957, it crossed the Atlantic Ocean in 53 days. The original* Mayflower *that brought the Pilgrims to Plymouth in 1620 took 66 days to cross what William Bradford called that "vast and furious ocean."*

were in Plymouth, his opinions back in Salem soon became all too evident.

If Williams could not start an argument, he could heartily join in arguments already under way. For the next two years in Salem, 1633 to 1635, he in fact did both. One argument in progress concerned the matter of women wearing veils in church, an argument from a question the apostle Paul had put to the church in Corinth: "Is it proper that a woman pray unto God with her head uncovered?" (I Corinthians 11:13). A Salem pastor, well before Williams's return to that village, had answered that question in the negative: No, it was not fitting for a woman to pray unveiled. Williams joined the negative, and Boston plunged into the debate. A newly arrived minister, John Cotton, felt that this question related mainly to local customs in Corinth. In Massachusetts, far removed in both space and time, veiling of women was not required, he announced in Boston, and he journeyed to Salem to make the same point. But of course that hardly settled the matter; the issue only got lost in more disputes coming to a boil.

The English flag at the time included a red cross that had been given to the king of England by the pope as a promise of victory in battle. A papal cross in a Puritan flag? To some people in Salem this made no sense, so they proceeded to cut the cross, or a part of it, out of the flag. But defacing and desecrating the national flag? To a good many others, that made no sense; it might even be treason. So the General Court (an executive, legislative, and judicial body) of the Massachusetts Bay Colony rebuked those who acted rashly and "without discretion" in defacing the flag. The rebuke was directly chiefly at John Endicott, the political leader in Salem. Roger Williams was not mentioned in the condemnation, but all Boston knew he was there in Salem, and wherever controversy erupted he must surely be involved.

On other issues, far more weighty than veils and flags, Williams left no doubt concerning his involvement. Indeed, he led the battle charge. Williams raised serious charges concerning the legal title—a grant or "patent"—of the land given by King Charles I to the Bay Colony. In doing this, Williams questioned the very foundation of the colony's government and legitimacy. Williams was especially troubled by the use of the Christian religion to do a very unchristian deed: namely, deprive the Indians of their own property without due compensation or negotiation. While in Plymouth, Williams had spent time among the Indians and had learned some of their languages and much of their culture. And he realized that they too had rights. English colonization, Williams argued, was "a sin of unjust usurpation upon others' possessions." Christian kings somehow believe that they are invested with right, by virtue of their Christianity, "to take and give away the Lands and Countries of other men." What nonsense, what absurdity!

From the point of view of the General Court, however, what horror, what treachery! Williams, summoned before the Court, was asked whether or not he was a loyal subject of King Charles. Did he intend to challenge the authority of the king himself? Did he propose treason, or perhaps revolution? Williams responded, rather mildly for him, that his argument was moral and religious rather than legal or political. And some ministers argued on his behalf that the tract, or statement, he had written on the matter (which no longer survives) was in places ambiguous or "obscure." No charges were levied against him.

But the citizens of Massachusetts were shaken. Was their land not even rightfully their own? Governor John Winthrop responded that land which "lies common, and hath never been replenished or subdued is free to any that possess or improve it." He added that, with respect to the Indians, "if we leave them sufficient for their use, we may lawfully take the rest, there being more than enough for them and us." And pastor John Cotton declared, with some wonderment, "We did not conceive that it is a just title to so vast a continent, to make no other improvement on millions of acres in it, but only to burn it up for pastime." On this question, the clash of cultures, settler and Indian, could not have been more obvious; unhappily, that clash replayed itself in America's history time and again, over the following decades and centuries.

Between Roger Williams and the General Court there had been something of a standoff. Matters might have quietly rested there, if only Williams had left well enough alone. But this he could never quite manage to do. Other matters of Massachusetts policy and procedure continued to trouble him. For example, the Bay Colony required all male inhabitants of 16 years of age or older to swear an oath of allegiance to the colony and the Crown, concluding with the words, "so help me God." But what if the swearer did not believe in God? It made no sense to require an unbeliever to swear by Almighty God, said Williams, though he persuaded few in the 17th century and would convince even fewer in later centuries, or so it seems.

Then there was the matter of the duties of the magistrates or civil officers. Did those public officials have a right to enforce such religious duties, as, for example, going to church or keeping the Sabbath day holy? Or, to put it in the language of the day, could the magistrate command obedience to the "first tablet" of the Ten Commandments? These commandments (loving God, avoiding idolatry, not taking the Lord's name in vain, keeping the Sabbath) pertained to the religious order, not the civil order (as the commandments of the "second tablet" did: not stealing, murdering, lying, or committing adultery). But should not the civil and religious orders reinforce and mutually support each other? Almost everyone in the first half of the 17th century in Europe and America answered that question with a "yes." Roger Williams answered it with a "no." He was an irritant, surely, but maybe far more than that.

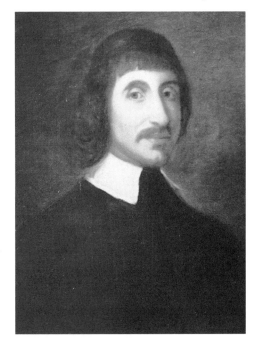

John Winthrop, first and frequent governor of the Massachusetts Bay Colony, was sometimes Roger Williams's friend and sometimes his foe.

Meanwhile, Williams had been appointed to pastoral duties in the church at Salem. This gave his opinions more status and the flavor of legitimacy. Technically, the Boston authorities could not remove him from a church office in Salem. Politically, however, they had other weapons at their disposal. Salem had applied to the General Court for an additional grant of land. The court thought that, under the circumstances, it made sense to wait on granting that petition until the pressing matter of Roger Williams had been settled. On July 8, 1635, Williams, called before the court once more, was officially warned that his opinions were "erroneous and very dangerous." A warning shot had been fired across his bow. A prudent man would have trimmed his sails and changed his course. Williams, more a man of principle than of prudence, did neither. The moment he won one concession or compromise, he quickly moved on to another position, more extreme, more "dangerous," as the court declared.

Though Williams regarded the court's treatment of himself as unfair, he was even more upset by its riding roughshod over Salem and that church. On behalf of the church in Salem, he wrote in late July to the "Elders of the Church at Boston," protesting their lack of Christian charity. Congregations should at least respect, if not love, each other, he argued. The Salem church had earlier written to the Boston church on their side of the argument concerning Williams, but the Boston church's elders had refused even to read that brotherly letter to its own members. If Williams could not find justice with the General Court, he should be able to "find a wisdom greater than theirs" within the church itself. But he and his church had been rebuffed. Was there not a rule of Christ to be considered, as much as a rule of a Massachusetts Court? Should the disputing parties not all come together, "for the presence of our souls and bodies together in the presence of the Lord is a gift"? "... To punish two or three hundred of our town for the conceived failing of the Church," and to do so before meeting together according to the New Testament rules, was a great evil. Williams concluded, we do not protest any civil matter; rather, "we speak of a spiritual offence against our Lord Jesus."

This appeal to the Boston church, presumably an entity separate from the Boston court, failed to change views in either church or court. In August and September, the parties' respective positions only hardened. Though Roger Williams fell ill, he neither moderated his tone nor shifted his course. For its part, the General Court had been as patient as it felt it could be. But its patience had now run out. Williams, moreover, was losing his following. Many of those who had defended or excused him did so no longer. Even the Salem church was now divided by some of those "dangerous opinions." And so on October 8, 1635, Williams was summoned once more to appear before the court.

The court decided to give Williams a final chance to recant: to take back what he had preached or written. They even sent the learned clergyman Thomas Hooker (later the founder of Connecticut) to spend much of a day and evening with him. But Williams could not be persuaded that he was wrong. Stubborn, yes—but not wrong. And so he went back to the court the next morning, October 9, of the same mind and heart. Similarly, the court could not be persuaded that it was wrong. And so, most solemnly, the court began: "Whereas Mr. Roger Williams, one of the elders of the church at Salem, hath broached & divulged diverse new & dangerous opinions..." This "whereas" was followed by several others that charged him with defying and defaming both the clergy and the magistrates. From there the court moved to the inevitable climax: "It is therefore ordered, that the said Mr. Williams shall depart out of this jurisdiction within six weeks."

Exile, expulsion, rejection. Where would Williams go? With a wife and a second child born this very October (the first had been born in Salem two years before), how could he and they survive? They could not safely return to England, for the Puritans had themselves found the environment there increasingly hostile. And if Williams had become too "dangerous" even for the Puritans, surely King Charles and his persecuting archbishop, William Laud, would hardly welcome him with open arms. With open prison gates, more likely. Nor could he hope for refuge in Plymouth Colony, for were it to harbor him as a fugitive, the wrath of the Massachusetts Bay Colony would certainly turn against it. What option remained? To escape into the wilderness, beyond the reach of the General Court, and far beyond the warmth of an English home.

When the Court granted Williams six weeks to prepare for his departure from their midst, it stipulated that he was not to go about drawing others into the black pool of his dangerous opinions. Williams met that stipulation so far as any public preaching was concerned. But those who called at his home learned that he had not changed his mind at all. So his presence continued to fester. By January, when he showed no sign of leaving and certainly no sign of repenting, the court decided that he must, without further delay, be placed upon a ship then in Boston harbor that was bound for England. From friends, Williams learned of this plan and knew that it promised only greater peril for him. Therefore, he determined not to be bound over, like a prisoner, to the ship's captain for a winter voyage to England. He would run.

When the arresting officers arrived at the home of Roger and Mary Williams, "they found that he had been gone three days before; but whither they could not learn." No one could have told them "whither," for Williams himself hardly knew. He would wander for 14 weeks in bitter snow and a "howling wilderness," not knowing what "bed or bread did mean." He had been thrown out by the English; he was taken in by the Indians. At length he came to the headwaters of the Narragansett, about 40 miles southwest of Boston. There he purchased some land from the Indians— with no patent or title from the king. And there he named the tiny settlement "Providence," as he later reported, with a "sense of God's merciful providence to me in my distress."

Near a "sweet spring," as he called it, he started building a shelter. By the spring of 1637 he could send for his wife and two small children to join him. Along with other friends and neighbors from Salem, the community grew to perhaps a dozen families, who began immediately to plant seed for crops that could sustain them by the fall.

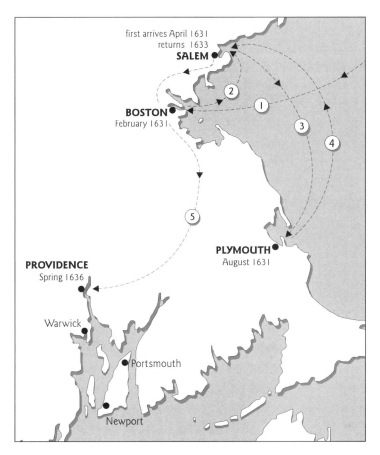

first arrives April 1631
returns 1633
SALEM ●

BOSTON ●
February 1631

PROVIDENCE
Spring 1636 ●

Warwick ●

● Portsmouth

Newport ●

PLYMOUTH ●
August 1631

This map plots the several moves that Williams made in his first five years in New England: from Boston to Salem to Plymouth; then back to Salem; and finally to Providence in 1636.

Meanwhile, friendly Indians offered some foodstuffs, while Williams borrowed money against his house back in Salem in order to purchase hoes and axes. By 1640 nearly 40 families had arrived—enough to begin taking steps toward forming some kind of simple government. That civil government would be carefully separated from the religious order. The founding members, moreover, declared in 1640: "We agree, As formerly hath been the liberties of the Town, so still to hold forth Liberty of Conscience." To some, guaranteeing liberty of conscience may have seemed a small victory; to Roger Williams, this was what his struggle, his exile, his torment were all about.

Making clear what his life was all about occupied Williams in the early months in Providence as he exchanged letters

ROGER WILLIAMS AND JOHN WINTHROP SEEK AN UNDERSTANDING

After the banishment of Roger Williams in 1635, he and John Winthrop exchanged several letters in an effort to explain themselves to each other. Though much of this correspondence has been lost, one letter from Williams to Winthrop, dated October 24, 1636, has survived. In this selection Williams responds to questions that Winthrop had raised.

Your first query, then, is this: "What have you gained by your new-found practices?"

I confess my gains counted up in man's exchange are loss of friends, esteem, maintenance, etc. But what was "gain" in that respect, I desire to count loss for the excellence of the knowledge of Christ Jesus, my Lord....

To your second query: "Is your spirit as even [calm] as it was seven years [ago]?" I will not follow the fashion either in commending or condemning myself. You and I stand at one dreadful tribunal [the Judgment Day]. Yet, what is passed I desire to forget, and to press forward toward the mark, for the prize of the high calling of God in Christ.

As for the evenness of my spirit: Toward the Lord I hope I more long to know and do his holy pleasure only; and to be ready not only to be banished, but to die in New England for the name of the Lord Jesus....

Sir, your fifth [query] is: "From what spirit and to what do you drive?"

Concerning my spirit, as I said before, I could declaim against it, but whether [that spirit] is the spirit of Christ, for whose visible kingdom and ordinances I witness, or the spirit of Antichrist (I John 4) against whom only I do contest, do drive me, let the Father of Spirits be pleased to search. And, worthy Sir, be you also pleased by the word [scripture] to search; and I hope you will find that you can say... "I also seek Jesus who was nailed to the gallows." I ask the way to lost Zion; I witness what I believe; I seek patiently (the Lord assisting) in sackcloth; I long for the bright appearance of the Lord Jesus.

with the Boston pastor John Cotton. Cotton, who had earlier defended Williams, came eventually to see that Williams really was "dangerous." One could never meet Williams halfway, or agree with him in part. It was all or nothing. Unfortunately, some of those earliest letters have been lost. Enough historical evidence has survived, however, to piece together the fundamental points of disagreement.

Although Cotton and Williams would argue vigorously and at great length against each other, they agreed on many large points. Both were Christians, both were Protestants, both accepted the authority of the Bible, both were graduates of Cambridge University, both were learned clergymen, and both were Puritans—though Williams was clearly the more "restless" of the two. Indeed, Williams recognized this trait when, years later, he spoke of the "restless unsatisfiedness of my soul." Positions vigorously defended today often became mere stopping points on his own "pilgrim's progress." Loyalty to Christ and loyalty to truth seemed always more a quest than a conquest. But he would press on, doggedly, earnestly, and—in the minds of many—perversely.

Remarkably, Williams and Cotton could agree about where their disagreements lay. Four large points divided them. First, in Cotton's words, "that we have not our land by patent from the King, but that the Natives are the true owners of it, and that we ought to repent" for thinking that this land was the king's to give. Williams could not have stated it more fairly himself. This, indeed, did lie at the very heart of his challenge to the political authorities of the Bay Colony. The English were not landowners, they were trespassers. And if the English felt strongly about property rights, so did the Native Americans. For Williams, this was simple truth. But for Cotton this was yet another sign of how cleverly the devil can deceive. "It is no new thing with Satan to transform himself into an Angel of light, and to cheer the soul with false peace, and with flashes of counterfeit consolation." In other words, Williams's conviction was simply a trick of the devil.

Second, Cotton deplored Williams's claim that an oath sworn in court should be required of only godly persons, of believers. Williams's problem, or one of them, was that he had an unfortunate tendency to take every idea to its extreme. "You overheated yourself," said Cotton, "in reasoning and disputing against the light" of God's truth. Cotton even regarded an illness that struck Williams in 1635 as God's judgment upon him. But, instead of being chastened, "you chose rather to persist in your way, and to protest against all the Churches and Brethren that stood in your way." The illness that God sent should have humbled you, Cotton argued, but it only hardened you. Williams, on the other hand, contended that making an unbeliever say "so help me God" forced that person (who did not believe in God) to take "the name of the Lord, thy God, in vain"— which the Third Commandment expressly prohibited.

Third, Cotton continued, Williams would have us renounce and denounce the Church of England in every respect. Here he issued his sharpest challenge to the ecclesiastical authorities. Williams would, Cotton complained, have us "bewail, repent, come out of the false Church's ministry." If Williams spots a sore on a man's leg, he immediately calls for an amputation! He does not know how to move gradually, moderately, peacefully. "We deny," Cotton wrote in a 1636 letter to Williams, "that it is necessary to Church fellowship...that the members admitted thereunto should all of them see, expressly bewail all the pollutions which they have been defiled with in the former church fellowship," that is, the Church of England. It is enough that they have condemned some errors, and by removing to the New World are now attempting to create a church more faithful to the New Testament. Even the apostle Paul was willing to work with those still "weak in the faith" and help them to grow more fully in their understanding of what the full gospel requires.

Williams, of course, saw this moderation as fateful compromise and unforgivable hypocrisy. One cannot find, he insisted, a middle ground between Christ and the Antichrist, between loyalty and disloyalty. And yes, sometimes surgery is required if the sore turns into gangrene and threatens the health of the entire body. If the Massachusetts Puritans believed that it was necessary to separate from the rule of bishops, from the demands of the Book of Common Prayer, and from the "prostitution of the ordinances of Christ," then those same principles should carry them steadily on to all

separation of "holy from unholy, penitent from impenitent, godly from ungodly." Well, replied Cotton, you seem determined to "impose a burden on the Church of Christ, which Christ never required at their hands nor yours."

Fourth and finally, Cotton saw nothing but calamity and social anarchy in Williams's bald assertion that the civil magistrate should simply leave religion alone. The magistrate's authority, to hear Williams talk, did not extend to matters of faith, to matters of conscience. True, replied Williams, his authority does not reach into the realm of the sacred. The distinction between the church and the world must always be kept clear; otherwise the "wilderness of the world" will invade the "garden of the church." One must keep a wall or a hedge between the secular and the sacred. This raises the whole matter of religious persecution on the one hand and religious liberty on the other, an issue to which both men give their full attention.

Apart from these four specific points of disagreement between Cotton and Williams, the root of the difficulty lay

John Cotton, a prominent Puritan minister in Boston, proved to be the leading antagonist of Roger Williams on the burning issues of religious liberty and the proper ties between church and state.

in the "holier than thou" complex manifest in Williams. Or so Cotton believed. Williams would, he said, be purer than anyone else, his church more "separate" than anyone else's, his allegiance to the New Testament more nearly perfect than that of other faithful Christians. And he would never listen to any reasonings that did not spring out of his own brain. The truth is, Mr. Williams, that the General Court did not banish you: you banished yourself. Well, in some respects, that may be true, conceded Williams. "If Mr. Cotton means my own voluntary withdrawing from those churches resolved to continue" in their evil and polluted practices of worship, yes, that was my decision.

If, on the other hand, Cotton would claim that my sentence of exile, my banishment from "common earth and air," was self-inflicted, he could not be more wrong. That wicked argument has been used against Christian martyrs down through the ages. We do not burn or hang or slay you: "it is your schism, heresy, obstinacy" that is responsible. Or, at best, it is the fault of the Devil who deceived you, but ultimately your fault for allowing the Devil to have his way with you. Besides, Cotton talked as though my civil banishment was a religious punishment, like being exiled from the church. And it is no wonder that he should talk this way, for in Massachusetts the church and the state are the same. "The Commonweal and Church is yet but one, and he that is banished from the one, must necessarily be banished from the other also." John Cotton has made my point, said Williams, and I rest my case. Cotton simply does not know, does not understand, what the separation of the church from the state is all about.

Cotton's fellow citizens had no difficulty agreeing that the Boston pastor had the best of the argument. After all, he was dealing with a man who kept changing his tune and his direction. He was, exclaimed one contemporary, like a weathervane, moving with every shift of wind, "constant only in his inconstancy." Or, changing the figure, another

Bay Colony citizen said that Williams was like a small craft that carried too large and high a sail; it was, therefore, "apt to overset in the stream, and ruin those that are embarked with him." He added, to make matters perfectly clear, that Williams was "a man of a very self-conceited, unquiet, turbulent, and uncharitable spirit." Some even called him "divinely mad." And Cotton himself explained that while the sentence of banishment was "neither done by my counsel or consent...I dare not deny the sentence passed to be righteous in the eyes of God."

Williams's enemies did not, however, have the last word. Although Rhode Island prospered slowly, it hung on to become the safest refuge for liberty of conscience. Dissenters of all stripes, persons of all religious persuasions or none, could find sanctuary in Rhode Island. Beside that "sweet spring," Williams sowed the seeds of a sweet liberty. He also came to the defense of Native Americans who had not surrendered their lands and would not, if it pleased God, have to surrender their lives.

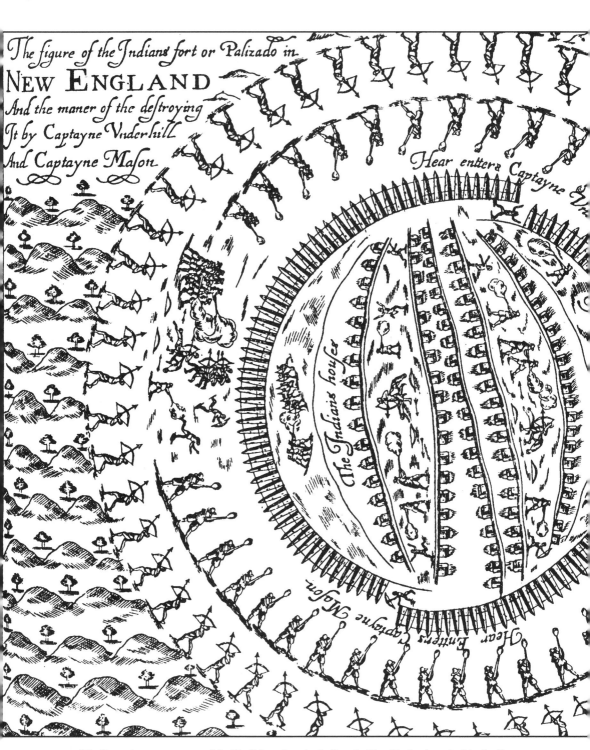

The first serious engagement of the English against the Indians in New England resulted in the Pequot War, 1637–38. This diagram shows the points of entry into the Indian fort by the English, at top and bottom. So devastating were the English attacks that the entire Pequot tribe was destroyed.

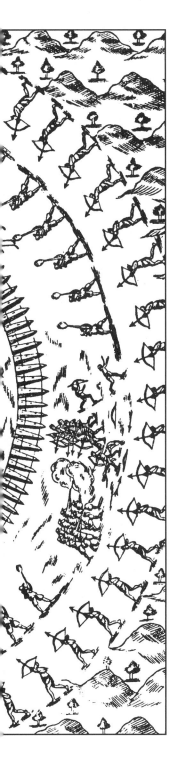

CHAPTER

2

WITH THE NATIVE AMERICANS

While still in his twenties, Roger Williams began a series of close contacts with the American Indians. His two years in the Plymouth Colony, from 1631 to 1633, gave him time to work out some theological problems, to welcome his firstborn (a son) into the world, and to begin a friendship with the Indians. "Friendship" was not the word usually applied to the relations between the English and the Indians, but Williams was the exception here, as in many other respects.

He also took the time and the trouble—as few other English did—to learn the Indians' languages. This skill proved to be of enormous value to him in matters of trade, diplomacy, anthropology, and most of all, cultural awareness. It was during his Plymouth Colony years that he first began to see the whole colonization enterprise from the Indians' point of view. And from that perspective England's claim (in the person of King Charles I) to ownership of land that the Indians had lived on for hundreds of years struck a false note. When he tried to persuade the Massachusetts Bay Colony to see the "land question" from the point of view of the Indian, he ran into major difficulties. Neither

31

John Winthrop nor John Cotton thought that the Indian point of view had much to recommend it. King Charles spoke for them—and for most other Englishmen up and down the Atlantic seaboard as well.

So when in 1636 Williams began to create a settlement and colony of his own at Providence, he strove to deal fairly with the Native Americans on the crucial issue of land. To obtain land for himself and his family, he first acquired a small acreage from the Indian chief (or sachem), Massasoit, of the Wampanoag tribe. In this and future transactions, Williams insisted that Indian customs and claims be followed, and that everyone agree to fair purchase prices. Even with the best of intentions, however, it was not always possible to avoid misunderstandings, or to find a precise line between competing claims. Williams understood that the power of the sachems was not absolute, that even chiefs had to consult with their subjects. But sometimes kinship had more force than the political structure of a tribe. Persons could even forsake the authority of one sachem for another, so that title disputes became inevitable. Even as Williams struggled to keep the lines of authority and legitimacy clear, so did the sachems themselves struggle to keep the loyalty of their subjects firm.

Then there were the English: they too had claims. When Williams first settled on the land he acquired from Massasoit, he learned from the Plymouth Colony that he had actually settled within the southern limits of their boundaries. The Plymouth governor "lovingly advised me," Williams wrote, that he should cross to the other side of the Seekonk River, where he would be out of their territorial claim. Williams promptly crossed over that river, putting him out of the Plymouth Colony and farther from the reach of the Bay Colony. This move placed him now, however, in lands that the Narraganset tribe ruled. Negotiating with their sachems Canonicus and Miantonomo, he at last found a more secure site near that "sweet spring" at the

head of the Narragansett Bay. Canonicus refused payment, but continued throughout his life (he died in 1647) to accept goods and gifts from Roger Williams. Just prior to his death, the aged chief asked that he be buried with cloth from Williams; this cloth was to be the last of many gifts to Canonicus over the years. He also asked that Williams attend his funeral, for the chief loved him as a son, Williams noted, "to his last gasp." On Williams's part, he added that "when the hearts of my countrymen and friends failed me," then the "infinite wisdom and merits" of Canonicus sustained him. Friendship: if only such warm relationships between the Indian and the English could have been multiplied a hundred times over.

But it could not be and was not. Soon after William's family joined him in Providence, tensions arose between

After his initial diplomatic efforts among the Narraganset Indians, Williams encouraged some Salem neighbors to join him in Providence. No contemporary sketch of this landing survives, but this 19th-century painting offers one artist's notion of what it might have been like.

the Massachusetts Bay Colony and the Pequot Indians. And though the Bay Colony had exiled Roger Williams, they now found it urgent to call upon his services as negotiator and diplomat, for Williams knew the Indians better than the citizens around Boston did, and he had earned their trust better than they had. Though Governor John Winthrop had voted for Williams's banishment, the two men, remarkably, maintained warm relations until the mid-1640s. Winthrop valued Williams's assistance in many matters, from the raising of goats together on an island in Narragansett Bay to being his eyes and ears regarding the movements and intentions of the Indians.

In July 1636, an English trader was killed off Block Island. Winthrop first suspected the Narragansets of the deed, but through the intercession of Williams and others he was persuaded that this was not the case. The Pequots were judged responsible. So Massachusetts planned an armed expedition against their strongholds. In late August of that same year, Williams wrote to Winthrop ("Much honored Sir") that "the Pequots hear of your preparations." But they felt secure, because one of their shamans (or "witches") promised to sink the Bay Colony's ships by "diving under water and making holes" in them below the waterline. The Pequots also dreamed of capturing a great many guns from those moving against them, "but I hope their dreams through the mercy of [the] Lord shall vanish."

Their dreams did not vanish, but their kingdom did. First, through labored negotiations Roger Williams persuaded the Narragansets not only to sever all ties with the Pequots but even to join with soldiers from the Bay Colony in attacking them. When the General Court in Boston hurriedly wrote Williams to do his best to break the alliance between the Narragansets and the Pequots, Williams, scarcely taking time to bid his wife good-bye, jumped in a "poor canoe" to row all by himself through "a stormy wind 30 miles in great seas, every minute in hazard of life" to the home of Canonicus. There, for three days and nights, he bargained with the Narragansets. He also met with, and even lodged with, ambassadors from the Pequots, who "reeked with the blood of my countrymen, murdered and massacred by them on [the] Connecticut River." Williams added, "I could not but nightly look for their bloody knives at my own throat also." Though he succeeded in making peace with the Narragansets, he failed to do so with the Pequots.

Blood had been shed on both sides, and more would soon pour forth. A combined force of Connecticut militia, Mohegans, and Narragansets attacked the Pequot fort at Mystic, Connecticut, on May 26, 1637. After only an hour of fierce fighting, several hundred Pequots, including women and children, had lost their lives. But the English were not through. When reinforcements arrived from Massachusetts, the fleeing Pequots were pursued—to be

A 19th-century engraving suggests some of the brutality of the Pequot War. Thanks to the diplomatic efforts of Roger Williams, the Narraganset Indians did not support the Pequots, but allied themselves with the English.

35

killed or enslaved or sold to buyers in the West Indies. By the time the Pequot War formally ended in September 1638, the tribe as a political entity was finished. For almost half a century, a pervasive if uneasy peace existed between the Indians and the English in New England. In all this, the services of Roger Williams had been so valuable that he even heard rumors that some in Massachusetts considered "whether or no I had not merited not only to be recalled from banishment, but also to be honored with some remark of favor." But if Williams had some friends in Massachusetts, he had enemies in greater abundance. The banishment remained; the honor was never bestowed.

Perhaps as early as 1637, Williams undertook the role of a trader with the Indians. Near the present site of Wickford, Rhode Island (about 20 miles south of Providence), Williams established a trading post that, with major interruptions, he endeavored to maintain until near the end of his life. The site, laid out for him by his good friend Canonicus, was on a cove of the Narragansett Bay. This site gave Williams a great advantage for shipping goods to or receiving them from abroad. Williams traded cloth, seed, cooking utensils, and simple tools, but strongly resisted any trading in guns or munitions. This latter trade would have made more money for Williams, but it would have been a cruelty to his Indian clients. For the same reason, he declined to trade in strong liquors, except in small amounts to be used as medication during serious illnesses. The Indians bartered with furs, skins, pottery, and baskets for whatever Williams had that they wanted. Over the years, Williams expanded his trade to include the English to the north and the Dutch to the south (in New York, then called New Amsterdam). But throughout, in his capacity as an honest trader, Roger Williams concerned himself chiefly with the Indians.

In 1643, Williams found it necessary to leave his still small and vulnerable colony for a long voyage to London.

The primary reason for his trip was to secure firmer legal standing for Rhode Island. At the time of Williams's trip, the colony had no charter; moreover, Massachusetts from the north, Connecticut from the east, and the Dutch from the south looked upon Rhode Island's lands as ripe for picking, or plucking, or annexing. Without some recognition from the government in England, Aquidneck Island was exposed on all sides to stronger or hungrier forces.

But a secondary purpose guided Williams as well. He had, since the mid-1630s, been doing a good bit of writing, but Rhode Island had no presses capable of publishing a book. Boston did have such presses, but the city fathers were in no way disposed to print anything written by their banished, wayward brother. If Williams was to be published, therefore, his best opportunity awaited him in London. And so several treatises from his pen at last reached a wider public in 1643–44.

His first and most popular book concerned the Indians. Published in 1643, it was called *A Key into the Language of America*. The use of the word "language" suggests that it might be a dictionary, and that, in part, is the case. But it is much more than that. As its title page indicates, it is also an early and valuable example of cultural anthropology, or in Williams's words, "with brief Observations of the Customs, Manners, and Worships...in Peace and War, in Life and Death." This would seem to be quite enough, but Williams had still more to offer. He wanted also to include "Spiritual Observations, General and Particular, by the Author." These "observations," usually given in poetic form, were designed mainly to instruct the English, who had a tendency to think of themselves and their culture as vastly superior to anything the Indians might know or do. This attitude, said Williams, was folly, noting that his book would attempt to expose that unwarranted pride.

The *Key* made a great hit in London, for the English were burning with curiosity to know more about the

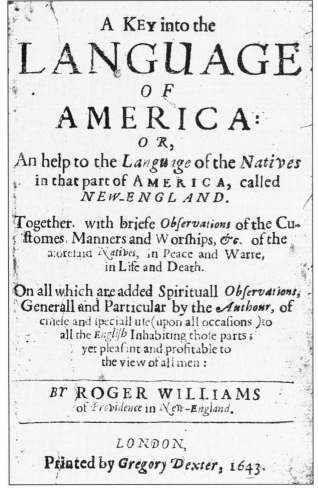

A KEY into the

LANGUAGE

O F

AMERICA:

O R,

An help to the *Language* of the *Natives*
in that part of A M E R I C A, called
NEW-ENGLAND.

Together, with briefe *Observations* of the Cu-
stomes, Manners and Worships, *&c.* of the
aforesaid *Natives,* in Peace and Warre,
in Life and Death.

On all which are added Spirituall *Observations,*
Generall and Particular by the *Authour,* of
chiefe and speciall use (upon all occasions) to
all the *English* Inhabiting those parts;
yet pleasant and profitable to
the view of all men:

BY ROGER WILLIAMS
of *Providence* in *New-England.*

LONDON,
Printed by *Gregory Dexter,* 1643.

Roger Williams's first and most popular book, both in England and America, this Key *continues to provide valuable insights into the culture of the early Narraganset Indians.*

North American "savages." Most of them had never seen an American Indian, and none of them had lived among them as Williams had. In addition, the book was written with a simplicity of style that quickly engaged the reader. Beyond that, it was written with "magnanimity, compassion, personal freedom and freshness," as an expert in American literature declared many decades ago. The logical progression of the book was from one's first encounter with an Indian ("of Salutations") to one's final resting place ("of Death and Burial"). Along the way, Williams provided Indian vocabulary, with aids to pronunciation, together with the English translation—something like a modern phrasebook for someone traveling in a foreign country.

Williams began his chapter on greetings with the observation that the Indians, like the English, are not all of one character or temperament: some are "rude and clownish," others are "sober and grave." Some will be the first to greet a stranger politely, while others will wait until they have been acknowledged first. There is nothing too surprising about any of this. And again, like the English, the Indians "are exceedingly delighted with being greeted in their own language." With Williams's *Key,* this became possible, particularly among the Narragansets, whose dialect makes up most of the vocabulary in the book. For example, if one wanted to ask an Indian, "How are you?", one would say, "Askuttaaquompsin?" And the Narranganset might well reply, "Asnpaumpmaûntam," that is, "I am very well." Of course, it might take a little practice to get this down just right—as would Spanish, German, French, or Japanese.

On the matter of personal names, Williams pointed out that these were largely for private rather than public use. Most of the time, one would address an Indian as "you" or "he" or "she." But when a sachem died, his personal name died with him. If another Indian happened to have the same personal name, he no longer used it, saying, "I have forgotten my name." The fact that the Indians had many expressions for hospitality, such as "Come hither, friend," or "Sit by the fire" indicates what Williams found to be true over and over: "They are remarkably free and courteous." They have hearts "sensible of kindnesses," leading Williams to conclude that "there is a savor of civility and courtesy even among these wild Americans, both amongst them-selves and towards strangers." Indeed, the English ("sons of God") could learn from them, as the author notes here in poetic form.

> If Nature's sons both wild and tame,
> Humane and courteous be;
> How ill becomes it sons of God
> To want [lack] humanity?

Williams's close observations are fully evident in a chap-ter entitled "Of Eating and Entertainment." Roasted corn or cornmeal was a staple of the Indian diet, in their own villages as well as when they were on the road. Williams once traveled with some 200 Indians for 100 miles or more, and all they carried in the way of food was their parched meal in a backpack or in a leather girdle around their mid-dle. This was sufficient to keep a man going for three or four days. "With a spoonful of this meal and a spoonful of water from the brook, have I made many a good dinner and supper," Williams reported. The English, however, preferred to have their meal with milk or butter, "which are mercies beyond the native's plain water."

For relief and refreshment, most Indians used tobacco. This plant was helpful in cases of toothache, "which is the only pain that will force their stout hearts to cry." But on long journeys they also resorted to tobacco "to revive and refresh them, they drinking nothing but water." If a stranger happened upon them while they ate, they would invite him in, "though but little enough prepared for themselves." And if they happened to have meat or fish, that too was freely shared. "It is a strange truth," Williams concluded, "that a man shall generally find more free entertainment and refreshing amongst these barbarians, than amongst thousands that call themselves Christians." Or, more poetically:

> Sometimes God gives them fish or flesh,
> Yet they're content without;
> And what comes in, they part to friends
> And strangers round about.

The Indians originally had no drums of their own, but they managed to make some in imitation of the English. And they had no horns, but bought a few from the Dutch. Their normal method of raising an alarm was simply to holler, and whoever heard this clamor passed it on along the line of small villages—sometimes as many as 100 in a distance of only 20 miles. The Indians slept on straw—lots of it—with no bedclothes. The fire served as their only cover: if the night was very cold, one "must be content to turn often to the fire." Whoever woke up first in the morning had the duty to "repair the fire." Here again, the behavior of the Indians came off better than that of the Europeans.

> I have known them leave their house and mat
> To lodge a friend or stranger,
> When Jews and Christians oft have sent
> Christ Jesus to the manger.

THE KEY TO UNLOCK MANY DOORS

In his popular and still useful Key into the Language of America *(1643),
Roger Williams introduced his treatise (from* The Complete Writings of
Roger Williams*) in this fashion.*

To my dear and well beloved friends and countrymen, in old and new
England:

I present you with a Key. I have not heard of the like, yet framed,
since it pleased God to bring that mighty continent of America to
light. Others of my countrymen have often, and excellently, and lately,
written of the country—and none that I know of beyond the goodness
and worth of it.

This key respects the native language of [that country], and happily
may unlock some rarities concerning the Natives themselves, not yet
discovered.

I drew the materials in a rude lump at sea, as a private help to my
own memory, that I might not by my present absence lightly lose what
I had so dearly bought in some few years hardships and burdens among
the barbarians. Yet, being reminded by some, what pity it [would be]
to bury those materials in my grave at land or sea; and [besides]
remembering how often I have been [asked] by worthy friends of all
sorts to afford them some helps this way, I resolved (by the assistance of
the most High) to cast those materials into this Key, pleasant and profitable for all, but especially for my friends residing in those parts.

A little Key may open a box, where lies a bunch of Keys.

In their villages, the Indians took the ties of kinship very seriously. If one of their number was slain, the next of kin had to seek revenge at all costs. Also, if the parents of young children died or were slain, the village as a whole immediately adopted the orphans as their own. And no beggars were to be found among them. Children were indulged—too much so, in Williams's opinion—with the result that most of them were "saucy, bold, and undutiful." If a village had been spared from sickness or plague (such as the European-imported smallpox), then commonly the number of children was large, for the natives "increase mightily."

The Indians frequently took more than one wife, Williams notes, and chiefly for two reasons. First, a "desire for riches," because each wife generally brought some possessions from her family, called a dowry, with her and because her labor in the fields increased the harvest for the husband, who only fished and hunted. Second, when a wife was pregnant, and for as long as a year after birth (as long as the child was "at the breast"), the wife kept apart from the husband. A second, third, or fourth wife was, therefore, a great convenience, though the Narragansets, Williams reported, generally took but one wife. Most Indians did not frown on sex before marriage, but adultery—both male and female—after marriage was severely punished. If a woman was adulterous, the husband took his revenge not upon her but upon the offending male: "before many witnesses, by many blows and wounds, and if it be to death, yet the guilty resists not, nor is his death revenged."

For the most part, Indian women bore their young without pain or complaint. Williams explained this first in terms of their hardy constitutions and second because of their continuous, heavy physical labors. They cultivated the fields, brought in the harvest, dug for clams and other shell-fish, and beat "all their corn in mortars." "Most of them count it a shame for a woman in travail to make complaint." Indeed, Williams reported, "I have often known in one quarter of an hour a woman merry in the house, and delivered, and merry again; and within two days abroad, and after four or five days at work." Indians uniformly honored the marriage bed, having no understanding of a religious demand for priests to remain unmarried.

Describing the physical bodies of the Indians, Williams made the point that all humankind was one. "Nature knows no difference," he wrote, "between Europeans and Americans [i.e., Indians] in blood, birth, bodies, etc., God having of one blood made mankind." This, of course, had implications for the relationships that should exist between peoples of different cultures or races, implications that found this poetic expression:

> Boast not proud English, of thy birth and blood,
> Thy brother Indian is by birth as Good.
> Of one blood God made him, and thee, and all,
> As wise, as fair, as strong, as personal [i.e., a
>   person with all the rights and dignity of a full
>   human being].

The natives lived in close touch with nature, day by day, month by month. They observed the seasons and had names for summer, fall, winter, and spring. They kept time, not as the English did, but by observing the sun and moon.

> They have no help of clock or watch,
> And Sun they overprize.
> Having these artificial helps, the Sun
> We unthankfully despise.

From childhood, the Indians learned the woods, the trails, the resting and hiding places. The English got lost in the vast wilderness, but rarely, Williams noted, did the Indians. "I have often been guided twenty, thirty, sometimes forty miles through the woods, a straight course," without any path or trail in sight. They also learned at an early age to run, and all did so. But some especially excellent runners could cover from 80 to 100 miles "in a summer's day." Within two days, the runner would be ready to retrace his steps. Despite all this, the Indians love to ride horses, but they owned very few because they could not afford the "English prices."

And so Williams wrote of the Indian view of the stars, of the winds and storms, of the earth and its fruits. He said they fed on geese, turkeys, cranes, and other fowl, which tended to be bountiful in all the bays, swamps, and inlets along the Atlantic shore. The birds were so abundant that special steps had to be taken to keep them out of the fields. Instead of scarecrows, the Indians lodged their older children

A painting of Ninigret, made for Governor John Winthrop, shows the leader of the Niantic Indians in full and formal dress. Winthrop and Ninigret conducted frequent negotiations aimed at preventing open warfare between the English and the Indians.

in small shelters around the corn. As day broke, the children knew their duty: scare the birds all away. Sometimes they even domesticated hawks, which were by nature well equipped to keep the other birds far from the fields. They also gathered nuts and berries, and if the corn crop failed, they gathered acorns that, after drying and boiling, became edible. Williams was especially ecstatic about the strawberries, reporting that God could have, but never did, make a better berry. The English, Williams reluctantly admits, put the strawberries and grapes to even better use by making fine wines, "as I have often tasted." But in fishing and hunting, the Indians excelled in their marksmanship and their nets.

Indians were more often naked than clothed, except for small aprons. Yet, said Williams, their behavior is modest and restrained. In fact, he added, "I could never discern that excess of scandalous sins amongst them, which Europe aboundeth with. Drunkenness and gluttony—generally they know not what sins they be." Observing the habits and manners of English traders who moved among them, the Indians had reason to feel some superiority of their own. As Williams wrote on their behalf:

> We wear no clothes, have many gods,
> And yet our sins are less;
> *You* are barbarians, pagans wild,
> *Your* land's the wilderness.

The Indians used seashells and beads for money, since they had no coins of their own. Sometimes, of course, they simply bartered, trading their furs or baskets for hoes or axes. They hung the strings of beads, or wampum, around their necks or wrists and "upon the necks and wrists of their wives and children." For trading, some Indian specialists concentrated only on the making of bows or arrows or dishes, the latter being an occupation chiefly of women. Indians who lived near the seashore collected shells in the summer, then made money out of the shells during the winter. In one of his few complaints against the Indians,

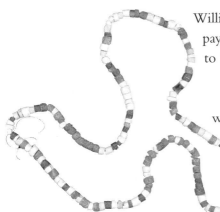

Wampum, made from beads or small seashells, served both as decoration and as a medium of exchange—in the absence of any coins or currency.

Williams noted that they were not prompt about paying their debts. Sometimes it was necessary to follow them "to their several abodes, towns, and houses, as I myself have been forced to do." Then Williams might have been met with the excuse that they had been ill and had been forced to pay the medicine man who came to heal them. Or they complained, as the English also did, that the price of goods changed from year to year, according to market demands that they hardly understood and were in no mood to accept as an explanation. Whoever deals with them, said Williams, must have wisdom, patience, and honesty, for the Indians were ever ready to say, "You deceive me." Furthermore, "They are marvelously subtle in their bargains to save a penny," and will run 20 miles or more to save a sixpence.

Given the training of Roger Williams at Cambridge University, as well as his intense involvement in matters religious, one would certainly expect him to observe with the keenest interest the religion of his neighboring Indians. And so he did. He counted the many names they had for God or the gods (37 in all), and noted how they saw divine power in any excellence observed around them. When Indians talked among themselves, Williams commented, they even spoke of such things as English ships, great buildings, iron plows, and books as indications of the divine spirit. "A strong conviction natural in the soul of man," Williams wrote, was "that God is—filling all things, and places, and that all excellencies dwell in God, and proceed from him."

The Indians held private ceremonies, or feasts, in times of sickness, drought, war, and famine throughout the year. But their great public feast came chiefly in the late fall, after all the harvest was in, and "a calm of peace, health, plenty, [and] prosperity" settled upon them. Then, as among the

Christians at Christmas, there was much joy and revelry and feasting. On other occasions, neighbors would give a feast and perhaps donate money on behalf of a person who was then obliged to call out loudly to the gods for "the health and prosperity of the party that gave it." Williams testified that he had often gathered with 20, 50, 100, or even "near a thousand persons at one of these Feasts." Perhaps because he was looking for it so intently, Williams even found a kind of religious freedom among the natives. "They have a modest religious persuasion not to disturb any man, either themselves, English, Dutch, or any in their conscience and worship."

Finally, Williams concludes his *Key* with attention to sickness, death, and burial among the Native Americans. In sickness, Williams was himself often called upon to render what assistance or comfort he could, "beyond my power," because they had few medicines at hand. But if a plague such as smallpox struck a village, all recognized that any cure was beyond their power or that of the English. Then the only option was to flee. "I have often seen a poor house left alone in the woods, all being fled, the living not able to bury the dead, so terrible is the apprehension of an infectious disease." For less serious illnesses, the Indians often resorted to a kind of sauna or "sweat lodge" that had been "exceedingly heated with a store of wood, laid upon a heap of stones in the middle." After a time, the fire was removed, but the stones stayed hot. At that point, 10 or 12 "enter at once, stark naked...here they do sit around these hot stones an hour or more, taking tobacco, discoursing, and sweating together." After that hour, "I have seen them run (summer and winter) into the brooks to cool them, without the least hurt."

Death was, for the natives as for all "natural men," the "King of Terrors." At the grave site, lamentations and tears were common. Often, bows and arrows or money would be placed in the grave to assist the dead in their transition to a better afterlife. "Sometimes a fair coat of skin [will be] hung upon the next tree to the grave, which none will touch, but [leave] it there to rot with the dead."

Williams even observed his aged friend Canonicus burn his own house and all within it when his son died, "as a kind of humble [appeasement] to the gods, who (as they believe) had taken his son from him." Williams concluded his work with a noble benediction, praying to the most high "and only wise God" and thanking him for the "wonderful supportment" that enabled Williams to study and converse with the Indians and "to frame this poor *Key*." He dared to hope and pray that his book would somehow open "doors of mercy to us and them," the first Americans.

In his introduction to the *Key*, Williams acknowledged that he had not addressed in it one class of questions: "What Indians have been converted? What have the English done in those parts? What hopes of the Indians receiving the knowledge of Christ?" Admitting that this was "the great inquiry" back in England, Williams indicated that he would soon "present you with a brief additional discourse concerning this Great Point." This tract, long lost from the collection of Williams's writing but finally rediscovered some 200 years after his death, is entitled *Christenings Make Not Christians.*

A good part of its message is contained in the title: a mere outward religious ritual does not alter the condition of one's heart. A christening or a baptism, to be sure, can be a powerful symbol, but it can also be an empty one if a life is not changed or set upon a new path. With regard to the Indians, who were generally unable to read the Bible and could not understand a creed or catechism without extensive tutoring, a so-called conversion might prove to be only an empty gesture. This was certainly true when conversion came at the point of a sword, as had so often been the case in earlier centuries. Williams denounced these "monstrous and most inhumane conversions" as a violation of the

Indians' spiritual integrity. What could be worse than this cruel practice of making Christians of thousands, "yea, tens of thousands by wiles and subtle devices, sometimes by force compelling them to submit to that which they understood not?" Williams would have none of it.

Therefore, though he knew the Indians better than most, though they trusted him more than they did most Englishmen, Williams decided that he would not seek to convert them. In this refusal he knew he would be misunderstood, and so he was. But his position was firm. "Woe be to me," he wrote, "if I call light darkness or darkness light. . . . Woe be to me if I call that conversion unto God, which is indeed subversion of the souls of millions in Christendom, from one false worship to another." Here Williams had in mind not only what was happening to native populations all over the world but the unhappy example of a West Germanic king in the Middle Ages who drove his army through a river, thereby "baptizing" them and making "Christians" of them all—in an instant. This charade made a mockery of everything that religion in general, or Christianity in particular, stood for.

Williams knew that forced conversion was no conversion at all. A required conformity or "some external submission" to a christening or a baptism or the observance of Sunday or formal prayers was no conversion at all. Worse, it possibly worked as a kind of inoculation or prevention against sincere religion. When a dominant culture or a powerful nation imposed its religion upon a weak and vulnerable people, it did not further the cause of Christianity; rather, it undermined it. The Native Americans, Williams believed, deserved better than religious persecution disguised as religious evangelism. What was to be done? Wait upon God, Williams replied. In accordance with God's own timetable, which is beyond our understanding, the time for the conversion of the Native Americans will finally arrive.

In the *Key*, Williams recounted a conversation with his

firm Indian friend, Canonicus. Williams learned that Canonicus, like all New England Indians, worried about the growing number of English arriving from abroad. And like many, he wondered if the English were dealing with the Indians—and himself—fairly. "In a solemn oration to myself, in a solemn assembly," Williams noted, Canonicus announced that he had never permitted "any wrong to be offered to the English since they landed, nor never will." Then, this "wise and peaceable prince," as Williams called him, added: "If the Englishman speak true, if he means truly, then shall I go to my grave in peace and hope that the English and my posterity shall live in love and peace together." Tragically, it was not to be.

When Canonicus and Williams conversed in the 1630s, the flow of English emigration to New England was still comparatively limited, and the occupation of lands in the Northeast was still relatively restricted. A half-century later, this was no longer the case. By then Massachusetts's inhabitants had pushed westward into the interior, settling on both sides of the Connecticut River. Some had moved northeast into what would become New Hampshire, others southwest into what would become Connecticut. Immigrants continued to pour in from abroad, and the English, no less than the Indians, managed to "increase mightily." More farms went into cultivation and more towns sprang from the soil. By the 1670s, more and more Indians concluded that the very ground was disappearing from under them. In the words of their leader, "I am determined not to live till I have no country."

That leader, Metacomet (known as "King Philip" to the English), was the son of Massasoit, the sachem of the Wampanoags around Plymouth. These were the people who had first sold land to Roger Williams, land that he later abandoned because it was within the borders of the Plymouth Colony. That was in 1636. Now, in the 1670s, rumors flew of Indian plots involving an armed attack against the English. When Metacomet worried and antagonized the English, Williams was once more called upon to take up his familiar role as diplomat and negotiator. At one point, he even gave himself up to the Wampanoags as a hostage to assure them that the Plymouth Colony would return their leader safely. Metacomet did return to his home, but only after surrendering some 70 guns in his possession. (In a mere half-century, guns had largely replaced bows and arrows among the Indians.) And Roger Williams was also allowed to return to his home safely.

But tensions and resentments continued to smoulder and build, especially in the Plymouth Colony. By 1675, rumors ran furiously once again: that Metacomet was rearming himself, that some major conflict was imminent.

In the bloodiest conflict by far between the English and the Indians, King Phillip's War, the English were ultimately victorious, but only after enormous cost in human life and property. This woodcut portrait of "King Philip," whose Indian name was Metacomet, was engraved in the next century by Paul Revere.

An Indian informer carried this word to the authorities at Plymouth; when the Wampanoags heard of this betrayal, they killed the messenger. Then, when Plymouth heard of that murder, they arrested three men suspected of the crime and condemned them to death. On June 13, Williams wrote to John Winthrop, Jr. (governor of Connecticut and son of Williams's now-deceased old friend from Massachusetts Bay): "Sir, it is true that Philip (fearing apprehension) stood upon his guard with armed barbarians." The Plymouth Court decided that it did not have sufficient evidence to put the three men to death, and so "let matters sleep." Williams hoped that at this point quiet would settle on the country.

He hoped in vain. For now, to complicate matters enormously, the Wampanoags moved to forge an alliance with the much larger, much stronger Narragansets—the old friends and trading partners of Roger Williams. The Massachusetts colony, upon hearing of this possibility, grew greatly alarmed. Representatives of the governor hurried to Providence to enlist Williams in a hastily arranged parley to keep the Narragansets at peace. Told of this mounting concern, the Narragansets informed Williams and the others that they "held no agreement with Philip in this rising against the English." They even promised that if Metacomet (Philip) or any of his men "fled to them, yet they would not receive them, but deliver them up unto the English." Had Williams succeeded again? Now in his seventies, he concluded a second letter, dated June 25, 1675, to John Winthrop, Jr., with these poignant words: "Sir, my old bones and eyes are weary with travel and writing to [governors] of Massachusetts and Rhode Island and now to yourselves."

But Williams had not succeeded. What historians now speak of as King Philip's War broke out only a few days later—with the Narragansets and others in league with the Wampanoags. The Indian attack was widespread, ferocious, and successful—beyond anyone's imagination—almost beyond the ability of the English to keep from being pushed back into the sea. Virtually all the frontier towns and villages were burned to the ground, with their inhabitants slain or scattered. Massachusetts pressed all able-bodied men from 16 to 60 into military service, promising bonuses of land in addition to their regular pay. Connecticut passed a law prohibiting any potential fighting man from leaving the colony. Even Roger Williams concluded that it was necessary for him to accept duty in the Rhode Island militia.

By December of 1675, Williams had lost all hope of being able to pour oil on very troubled waters. Negotiation had failed, diplomacy was done. To John Winthrop, Jr., he wrote on December 18 that "I presume you are satisfied in the necessity of these present hostilities, and trust that it is not possible at present to keep peace with these barbarous men of blood." They must, he felt, be dealt with as one deals with the wolves that attack a flock of sheep. In the winter, Williams found it necessary to send his own wife to the island of Aquidneck, where other Rhode Islanders had fled and where wounded soldiers were sent for convalescence. In late March, the native warriors attacked Providence, sending most of the buildings and houses up in flames, including Roger Williams's own home. The bonds forged decades earlier between Williams and Canonicus were forever broken.

In the number of lives lost and property ruined, King Philip's War was, in proportion to the population at that time, America's deadliest and costliest war. Massachusetts alone had casualties in the many hundreds, as did the Indians. Fifty-two of New England's 90 towns had suffered from attack; many were totally destroyed. "King Philip" himself was captured and killed on August 12, 1676, effectively bringing the bitter hostilities to an end. Now it was time to reestablish lines of commerce and replant the devastated fields. It was also time to rebuild towns and homes. Trust between the English and the Indians, however, could not be rebuilt.

Williams had expended himself and his property on behalf of the English with such sacrifice that Massachusetts was moved on March 31, 1676, to temporarily suspend his banishment as long as he refrained from "venting any of his different opinions." Those sacrifices had reduced him to poverty. He even had to beg the Massachusetts governor for writing paper, because he often found it necessary to write on "public business" and was "now near destitute." Whether Massachusetts ever responded to this sad request is not known.

RHODE-ISLAND

CHARTER,

Granted by King CHARLES II. in the Fourteenth Year of his Reign.

Quintadecima pars Patentium Anno Regni Regis CAROLI *Secundi Quintodecimo.*

CHARLES the Second, by the Grace of God, &c. To all to whom thefe Prefents fhall come, Greeting. Whereas We have been informed by the humble Petition of Our trufty and well beloved Subjects, John Clarke, on the behalf of Benjamin Arnold, William Brenton, William Codington, Nicolas Eafton, William Boulfton, John Porter, John Smith, Samuel Gorton, John Weekes, Roger Williams, Thomas Olaey, Gregory Dexter, John Cogefhall, Jofeph Clarke, Randall Houlden, John Greene, John Roome, Samuel Wildbore, William Field, James Barker, Richard Tew, Thomas Harris, and William Dyre, and the reft of the purchafers, and free inhabitants of Our Ifland called Rhode-Ifland, and the reft of the Colony of Providence Plantations, in the Narraganfet-Bay in New-England in America, That they purfuing with peace, and loyal minds, their fober, ferious, and religious intentions, of godly edifying themfelves, and one another, in the holy Chriftian faith and w rfhip as they were perfuaded, together with the gaining over and converfion of the poor ignorant Indian natives, in thofe parts of America, to the fincere profeffion and obedience of the fame faith and worfhip, did not only by the confent and good encouragement of Our royal progenitors, tranfport themfelves out of this kingdom of England into America; but alfo fince their arrival there, after their firft fettlement amongft other Our fubjects in thofe parts, for the avoiding of difcord, and thofe many evils which were likely to enfue upon thofe able to Our fubjects, not being able to bear in thofe remote parts their different apprehenfions in religious concernments; and in purfuance of the afo efaid ends, did once again leave their defirable ftations and habitations, and with exceffive la bour and travel, hazard and charge, did tranfplant themfelves into the mi ft of the Indians natives, who (as We are informed) a e the moft potent Princes and People of all that country; whereby the good Provi ence of Go (from whom the Plantations have taken their name) upon their labour and induftry, they have not only been preferved t admiration, but have increafed and profpere , and are feized and poffeffed, by purchafe and confent of the faid natives, to their full content, of fuch lands, iflands, rivers, harbours and roads, as are very convenient, both for plantations, and alfo for building of fhips, fupply of pipe-ftaves, and other merchan-

dize, and which lies very commodious in many refpects for commerce, and to accommodate our Southern plantations, and may much advance the trade of this Our realm, and greatly inlarge the territories thereof; they having by near neighbourhood to, and friendly Society with, the great body of the Narraganfet Indians, given them encouragement, of their own accord, to fubject themfelves, their people and lands, unto Us; whereby (as is hoped) there may in time, by the bleffing of God upon their endeavours, be laid a fure foundation of happinefs to all America : And whereas in their humble Addrefs. they have freely declared, That it is much on their hearts (if they be permitted) to hold forth a lively experiment, that a moft flourifhing civil ftate may ftand, and beft be maintained, and that among Our Englifh fubjects, with a full liberty in religious concernments, and that true piety, rightly grounded upon gofpel principles, will give the beft and greateft fecurity to Sovereignty, and will lay in the hearts of men the ftrongeft obligations to true loyalty : Now know ye, That We being willing to encourage the hopeful undertaking of Our faid loyal and loving fubjects, and to fecure them in the free exercife and enjoyment of all their civil and religious rights appertaining to them as Our loving fubjects; and to preferve unto them that liberty in the true Chriftian faith and worfhip of God, which they have fought with fo much travel, and with peaceable minds and loyal fubjection to Our royal progenitors, and Ourfelves, to enjoy : And becaufe fome of the people and inhabitants of the fame Colony cannot in their private opinion conform to the publick exercife of religion, according to the liturgy, form, and ceremonies of the Church of England, or take or fubfcribe the oaths and articles made and eftablifhed in that behalf; and for that the fame, by reafon of the remote diftances of thofe places, will, as We hope, be no breach of the unity and uniformity eftablifhed in this nation, have therefore thought fit, and do hereby publifh, grant, ordain and declare, That Our Royal Will and Pleafure is, That no perfon within the faid Colony, at any time hereafter, fhall be any-wife molefted, punifhed, difquieted, or called in queftion, for any differences in opinion in matters of religion, and do not actually difturb the civil peace of Our faid Colony; but that all and every perfon and perfons may, from time to time, and at

The hard-won charter of Rhode Island, granted in 1663, remained the foundation of that colony's government throughout the colonial period and well beyond. Its most distinctive feature, soon echoed in the charters of other colonies, was its guarantee of a "full liberty in religious concernments."

3

FOUNDER OF
RHODE ISLAND

During his five years in the Massachusetts and Plymouth colonies, Roger Williams was always the outsider: complaining about this or that practice, agitating for this or that reform. But as of the middle of 1636, he was the insider. Now he could not protest against the authorities, for suddenly he had become the authority. He had a town and a colony to run, and how did one do that anyway?

Williams had been banished into a wilderness. And a wilderness, by definition, has no trails or paths. In addition, however, no paths opened up before him in the matters of government for which he was now responsible. He could not keep running; he had a family to support; he had several causes to serve; somehow, he had to succeed. Some of the friends and neighbors from Salem who decided to join him in Providence could come and go as they pleased. Roger Williams could not—he had to make things work. And he knew it would not be easy. A few years later he wrote of this time as one filled only with "miseries, poverties, necessities, wants, debts, hardships of sea and land." That was not much of a foundation on which to build either a colony or a town.

So where should he start, and how should he begin? In the summer of 1636, he wrote to John Winthrop for advice, because Winthrop had by then been governing a colony for about six years. "I shall humbly crave your help," Williams freely acknowledged. For the town of Providence had no legal authorization from the king, or anyone else back in England. It certainly had no authorization from the Massachusetts Bay Colony, and at this point it lacked even a church structure that might have granted some stability and direction. In such a sea of uncertainty, Williams could only improvise. This, so far, is what we have done, he told Winthrop: "The masters of families have ordinarily met once a fortnight [every two weeks] and consulted about our common peace, watch, and planting." That is, decisions would be arrived at not by dictatorial authority but by mutual consent. All would have some obligation to join in the watch: that is, to be on guard against an Indian attack (especially from the Pequots) and to sound an alarm in the case of any other emergency, such as fire. Planting, of course, was most urgent, for the community of 30 or so persons could look only to itself for sowing seed and reaping a harvest.

The program was modest enough: let us work together as sensibly as we can, but let us work. Williams encouraged each head of a household to sign a covenant, or agreement, that would bind them to come together "with free and joint consent" and "to promise each unto other" that whatever the majority decided to do, all would obey. As new arrivals came, they, too, would be obliged to sign this agreement. One person would be named the town officer, whose duty it would be to call meetings and gather votes on the issues that came before them. Roger Williams was one of the first to serve in that capacity. The few surviving notes from the first years show him writing "in the name of the King and Parliament of England" in an effort to give some force or standing to these tentative steps toward self-government.

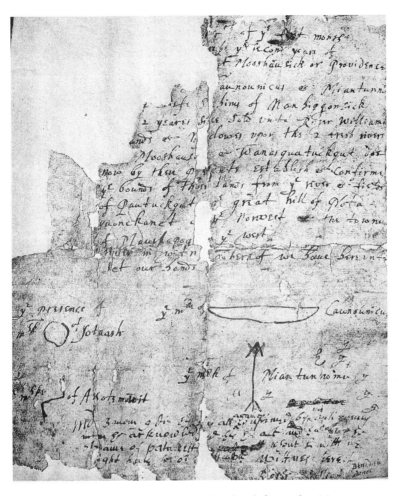

Roger Williams did not conquer the lands for his early settlement, but won them from the Indians through purchase and negotiation. The Narraganset chiefs signed the deed of transfer with a bow (Canonicus) and an arrow (Miantonomi). This fair exchange got Williams's relationship with the Indians off to a promising start.

Having acquired title to the land from the Narraganset Indian chiefs, in 1636 Williams proceeded to divide parcels of land among the first settlers. Each parcel was a narrow strip that began down by the spring, and then moved up the steep hill to its top. Williams's parcel was the same size as everyone else's. Few written records were kept of these earliest transactions, which only added to Williams's many difficulties in trying desperately to settle endless disputes about land. The English thirst for land, Williams observed, was very strong, as though they had just come from a "long and starving passage" at sea. They could not wait to set their feet on firm soil that they could call their own. Land,

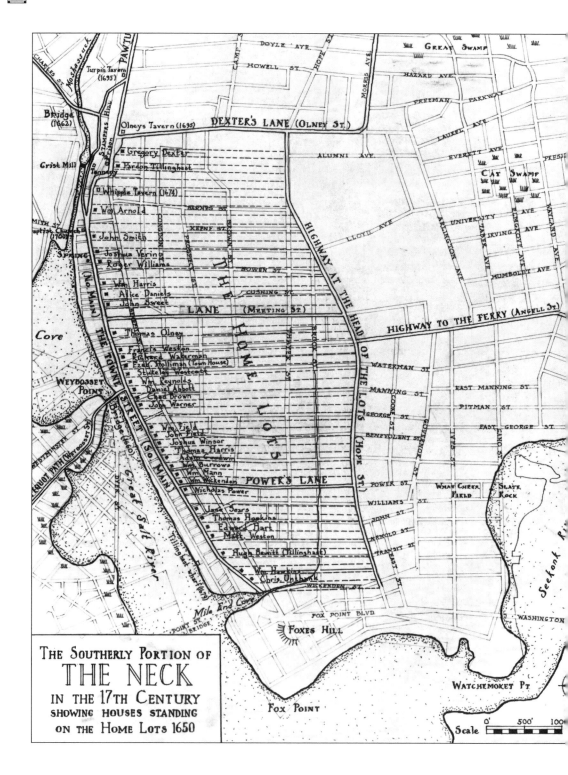

THE SOUTHERLY PORTION OF
THE NECK
IN THE 17TH CENTURY
SHOWING HOUSES STANDING
ON THE HOME LOTS 1650

Williams concluded, was one of the "gods of New England." Having seen the greed of so many, Williams—who certainly had the strongest claim of any to large parcels of land—carefully refrained from bowing down to that New England god. He never amassed land for himself, never feathered his own nest. As he wrote, "I desire not to sleep in security and dream of a nest which no hand can reach." From time to time, his wife no doubt would have wished for a little more thought about that safe and warm nest.

As Williams labored for some semblance of stable town government, he also recognized the necessity for stability in the church's organization. He had criticized the Puritan churches and described what seemed to him a better way for the church: complete separation from the Church of England and full separation of civil power from spiritual activity. For those moving into his colony, Williams had ordered that "no man should be molested for his conscience." But while this was a most valuable directive, it did not by itself provide any positive option of what to do with one's conscience as far as sacred worship was concerned. It was time for the town of Providence, only two years in the making, to have a church.

But what sort of church? Not the Church of England, of course, nor Puritan. What then? Attracted to the idea of separation and to those who in England had been persecuted for their separatism, Williams was further attracted to those who argued that one should come into a church only through her or his voluntary consent. Infants should not be baptized into a church that they had not chosen. Nor should people automatically be counted as members of a national or official church just because they lived in a certain territory or within the bounds of a specified parish. Baptism should be administered not to some bawling babe in arms as the Puritans did, but only to adult believers who had, voluntarily, offered a confession of their personal faith. In the first half of the 17th century, the English Baptists

The town plan on the preceding page shows the division of land among the first settlers in Providence. The long and narrow lots ran from the river and Town Street up the steep hill behind the home sites. All grants of land, including Roger Williams's, were of equal size.

came closest to the position that Roger Williams had staked
out. And in fact, his enemies in Massachusetts kept pushing
him into the Baptist camp as they charged him with various
departures from orthodoxy, or traditional Christian doctrine, associated with the name (or with the name
"Anabaptist," meaning rebaptizer, that Massachusetts regu-
larly preferred to use).

In 1638, Williams and 11 other settlers organized a
Baptist church in Providence—the first of that denomination in America. They had no building, but that was not
critical, for the church was the people, the congregation. A
building was only a "meetinghouse," never to be equated
with the real substance of a church—namely, its members.
One did not automatically become a member of the church
by moving to Providence, by acquiring land, or by voting or
paying taxes. Government pertained to "civil things only."
The church was entirely different, wholly separate. One had
to take the active and deliberate step of *choosing* to join the
church. One first made a confession of faith, then was baptized, and only after this was the man or woman received
into the fellowship or membership of the church. Like the
town itself, this church was a story of small beginnings.

Those beginnings seemed seriously threatened, not by
an outside force or a Bay Colony enemy, but by Roger
Williams himself. Ever restless, Williams kept searching his
Bible for evidence of the "true church." What he concluded, after only a few months in this Baptist church, was that
the true church must await the return of Christ to the
earth. Then Christ could appoint new apostles to take the
place of the apostles in the New Testament who had created
a pure church. But now the age of the apostles had passed,
and not until Christ returned to create new ones could a
genuine New Testament church come into being. If, therefore, no true church currently existed, this meant that even
the church in Providence did not measure up to the biblical
standard. So Williams left the church he had helped to

The First Baptist Church in Providence, founded by Williams and his neighbors in 1638, initially met in private homes. By 1775, however, the congregation was able to erect this handsome edifice—large enough to accommodate the students of Brown University for their commencement ceremony.

create. But the church endured, as did Williams's own interest in and support for that tiny knot of Baptist believers. He would continue to defend and inspire them in the cause of religious liberty.

Rhode Island itself soon became, if not an inspiration, at least a haven for those seeking refuge from persecution and repression. In Massachusetts Anne Hutchinson, a midwife and theologian, had dared to hold religious gatherings in her own home. Further, she had dared to lead theological discussions there that soon brought her to the attention of the Bay Colony authorities. They listened to many reports about her and did not like what they heard.

All Puritans agreed that salvation was a gift of God. It was God's choice, not man's or woman's, that made salvation possible. One could not earn, could not work for, could not merit salvation. Good works were, as the Bible said, "filthy rags" in the sight of the Lord. Grace—God's free gift of saving love—was all. Anne Hutchinson was on solid ground in proclaiming all this, steadily and boldly. The ground shifted a bit, however, when she went on to assert that because morality did not bring about salvation, then morality and religion were two separate matters. Just as one did not earn salvation by being moral, so one did not after salvation necessarily demonstrate a higher, more faithful, moral code. What Hutchinson came dangerously close to saying was that religion and morality had absolutely nothing to do with each other.

This idea challenged the foundation of the Puritan social order as seriously as Williams, in his charges about who really owned the land, challenged their political order. The magistrates of Massachusetts decided to warn Hutchinson as Williams had been warned. But Hutchinson, like Williams, paid little heed to warnings. So in November 1637 the General Court, with John Winthrop once more presiding, felt called upon to summon this radical to appear before them. Hutchinson had complained against the Bay Colony's ministers, including her own pastor, because they did not give sufficient emphasis to the all-sufficient power of God's grace. The court pointed out that she had said things "very prejudicial to the honor of the churches and the ministers thereof." She had disturbed the peace of the colony and had persisted in holding private meetings in her home. Such things, said Winthrop, were neither proper "in the sight of God nor fitting for your sex."

When asked by what authority she taught doctrines not supported by the colony's official teachers, Hutchinson replied, perilously, that private revelations had been granted to her. Hutchinson claimed she needed neither the Bible nor the ministry, for the Holy Spirit spoke directly to her. For those charged with maintaining an orderly society, this was terrifying indeed. This way all persons, male or female, could become their own authority, not bound by the counsel of their elders or their betters. The inevitable result would be not harmony but anarchy. This the court could not tolerate. The judgment was clear, as it had been with Roger Williams just two years earlier: "She shall be banished out of our liberties and imprisoned 'til she be sent away."

Banished, but to what place? When Williams had been banished, only wilderness awaited him. But Anne Hutchinson and her many followers had a better option: Rhode Island. With the help of Roger Williams, who interceded with the Indians, the followers of Hutchinson were able to purchase land on the largest island in Narragansett Bay, sometimes called Aquidneck and sometimes simply Rhode Island. In March 1638, some 80 householders, still in Boston, signed a civil compact "solemnly in the presence of Jehovah" to form themselves into "a body politic, & as He shall help will submit our persons, lives, and estates unto our Lord Jesus Christ, the King of Kings." Roger Williams indicated that he had many conversations with Anne Hutchinson, some on religious matters and others on the urgent matter of finding refuge. The town of Portsmouth, on the northern end of Aquidneck Island, became that refuge for Hutchinson and her large following.

With the creation of Portsmouth, Williams's colony was growing. The name of Providence or, later, Providence Plantations, would not

Roger Williams was not the only person to suffer at the hands of the Massachusetts Bay Colony. In 1637, Anne Hutchinson was exiled for her radical religious views and, like Williams, she fled to Rhode Island. This statue of her and her daughter now stands—perhaps by way of apology—on the grounds of the Massachusetts State House in Boston.

Roger Williams's friend and fellow minister, John Clarke of Newport, published in England a report of the continued persecution of Baptists by the authorities in Massachusetts Bay. Clarke identified himself here only as a "Physician of Rode Island in America," since these 17th-century Baptists believed one should not earn a living from preaching the gospel.

ILL NEWES

FROM

N E W - E N G L A N D :

OR

A Narative of *New-Englands*

P E R S E C U T I O N.

WHERIN IS DECLARED

That while old *England* is becoming new, *New-England* is become Old.

Also four Proposals to the Honoured Parliament and Councel of State, touching the way to *Propagate the Gospel of Christ* (with small charge and great safety) both in Old *England* and New.

Also four conclusions touching the faith and order of the Gospel of Christ out of his last Will and Testament, confirmed and justified.

By JOHN CLARK Physician of Rode Island in *America*.

Revel. 2. 25. *Hold fast till I come.*
3. 11. *Behold I come quickly.*
22. 20. *Amen, even so come Lord Jesus.*

L O N D O N,

Printed by *Henry Hills* living in *Fleet-Yard* next door to the *Rose* and *Crown*, in the year 1652.

4TH S. — VOL. II.   1

---

be sufficient to cover an ever enlarging enterprise. One year after the founding of Portsmouth, at the other end of Aquidneck Island, the town of Newport would appear. The major figure in the first decade or two of Newport's history was another clergyman, John Clarke. Clarke had left Massachusetts voluntarily, agreeing with Anne Hutchinson that the clergy there gave too much attention to "good works" and not enough to God's grace. In Newport Clarke organized America's second Baptist church. Unlike Williams, Clarke remained a Baptist all his life, even as he remained a stalwart defender of the rights of Rhode Island against the greedy land grabs of neighboring colonies.

Now three towns tried to enter into some governmental harmony: Providence, Portsmouth, and Newport. A fourth, Warwick, would soon join them. That addition was the work of Samuel Gorton, an abrasive and difficult spokesman. But if Williams maintained good relations with Anne Hutchinson and John Clarke, he failed to achieve that level of friendship with Gorton. Gorton had arrived in Massachusetts in 1636, just months after Williams had left. His singular opinions soon made him unwelcome there, so he drifted southward—as Williams had—to the Plymouth Colony. By 1638 he had worn out his welcome there and decided to cast his lot with the Hutchinson group in Portsmouth. But Gorton was a hard man to endure. He questioned all authority, civil or clerical, questioned the existence of heaven and hell, and denied the doctrine of the Trinity (traditionally defined as God the Father, God the Son, and God the Holy Spirit). He was jailed, whipped, and ultimately banished from the island of Aquidneck. That, of course, made Providence his obvious next stop.

Williams did not greet Gorton's arrival in early 1641 with joy. Quite the opposite, as his letter to John Winthrop in March 1641, makes clear: "Master Gorton, having foully abused high and low at Aquidneck, is now bewitching and bemaddening poor Providence." Gorton had attacked all authorities in the most abusive fashion and had attacked the ordinances of the church, baptism, and the Lord's Supper as improper and invalid. Williams, who was generally prepared to accept any dissenter or religious malcontent, drew the line at Gorton. He stood against Gorton's becoming a citizen of the town and against extending any of the privileges of the town to him. Gorton, he said, must first reform "his uncivil and inhumane practices at Portsmouth" before he could be accepted at Providence. If Gorton stayed, Williams strongly hinted that he would leave. But it was Gorton who left, first for England, where he persuaded the Earl of Warwick to defend his claims to a portion of Rhode Island around Shawomet, about 10 miles south of Providence. Then, returning to America in 1648, Gorton settled at Shawomet, which he promptly renamed Warwick in honor of his noble protector.

By this latter date, the colony of Rhode Island consisted of four towns: Providence, Portsmouth, Newport, and Warwick. Even more important, Rhode Island had by this time won from England its very own charter. In bringing about this achievement, the central figure, to no one's surprise, was Roger Williams. Recognizing that Rhode Island could have no peace from its neighbors and no domestic tranquility until its legal base was secure, Williams left for London in the summer of 1643. For him the most convenient route would have been to take a ship from Boston because no transatlantic vessels sailed from Providence. But Williams was still under the order of banishment in Massachusetts; to travel there would be to risk arrest that would delay or even cancel his mission. So, less conveniently, he made his way to New Amsterdam (now New York) to deal with the Dutch for his passage. That he knew the Dutch language certainly helped; by March he was aboard a ship bound for London. As the ship eased out of the harbor, Williams saw evidence of the warfare then under way between the Dutch and the Mohawks. "Mine eyes saw their flames at the town's end, and the flights and hurries of men, women, and children." Unhappily, among the victims of the Mohawk attack was Anne Hutchinson who, with some of her children, had by this time moved from Portsmouth to Long Island.

If New Amsterdam was in turmoil, Williams found an

England plunged into even greater strife. The forces of Parliament were arrayed against those of King Charles I in a bloody civil war. In June 1643, Parliament abandoned all pretext of loyalty to the king. Before the decade was over, the king was beheaded by order of Parliament, with Oliver Cromwell assuming power as the Great Protector. The middle of a civil war did not seem like a promising time for a tiny settlement 3,000 miles away to be asking for special attention and particular favor. However, many of Williams's old friends, long outside the centers of power, now exercised great influence

in Parliament. The Church of England and the king were at this point the outsiders: not calling the signals, not wielding their unchallenged swords, not persecuting or banishing. The worst of times for England might prove to be the best of times for Roger Williams.

And so he proceeded to lobby and persuade on behalf of his poor colony. He established a good relationship with Oliver Cromwell, the two men discussing such theological questions as when the world might come to an end and Christ return to earth. Other friends, such as Sir Henry Vane, shared with Roger Williams the "honor" of having been exiled from Massachusetts because of aligning himself with the party of Anne Hutchinson. But if Vane had lost power and prestige in Massachusetts, he gained both in London and in Parliament. As his fortunes rose, so did those

In 1641, Catholics in northern Ireland, fearful of a powerful and Protestant Parliament, massacred some 3,000 Protestants in Ulster. A "snapshot" of that bloody event is represented in this print. Before the decade ended, Oliver Cromwell and his army responded with a devastating slaughter of Irish Catholics in the same region—and well beyond.

of Williams as far as obtaining a charter for Rhode Island was concerned. Another friend, the poet John Milton, published a treatise calling for freedom of the press at the same time that Williams published his treatise calling for freedom of religion. Milton even recommended his own printer, Gregory Dexter, to Williams for this task. Williams liked Dexter and his work so much that he took him back to Rhode Island with him.

But not before getting that all-important charter. Charters were normally granted by the king or, at the very least, in the name of the king. But now no king sat on the throne. In this unusual circumstance, Williams turned to Parliament itself for his charter. After many months of political maneuvering and pleading, in March 1644 Parliament looked with favor upon the humble petition from Providence Plantations. Williams still had enemies, of course, even in England, but at this juncture he had even more friends. The crucial committee acted favorably, with only two votes to spare. Williams eagerly grasped the document delivered to him: "A Free Charter of Civil Incorporation and Government for the Providence Plantations in the Narragansett Bay in New England."

The name "Rhode Island" does not even appear in this title because the inhabitants of Portsmouth and Newport were still arguing about just what to call their island. But the charter did name those two towns, along with Providence, in the formal legal language of the day: "Whereas divers well-affected and industrious English inhabitants in the towns of Providence, Portsmouth, and Newport...have adventured to make a nearer neighborhood...and society to and with the great body of the Narragansets, which may in time, by the blessing of God upon their endeavors, lay a surer foundation of happiness to all America...."

This "whereas," followed by other such stipulations, led to the final and most welcome grant of a charter. The government thus incorporated was "civil": that is, nothing was said about the religious duties and responsibilities of the government, for it had none. Any state that Roger Williams had anything to do with would concern itself with secular, or civil, matters only.

When in 1657 English authorities wrote to the legislators of Rhode Island, asking for their help in stamping out the new sect of Quakers (radical Protestants who arose during Comwell's time), the General Assembly calmly replied: "We have no law among us whereby to punish any for only declaring...their minds and understanding concerning the things and ways of God, as to salvation and eternal condition." Just as Williams rejected the notion of a divine right of kings—that kings were empowered by God to rule—so he discarded the idea of a divine origin for government. Government came from the people; it arose from a covenant, a voluntary agreement, as in the first days in Providence. Government was good, a legitimate function of citizens banded together. But government had no special sanctity, and certainly no divinity.

With his precious parchment in hand, in August 1644 Roger Williams set sail for America. This time he could land in Boston because several powerful members of Parliament had given him a letter to the governor of Massachusetts, formally requesting that Williams be granted the right of safe passage from Boston back to the boundaries of Rhode Island. The letter also spoke, with sadness, of the disagreements between the Bay Colony and Williams, reminding all who would listen that they should not be enemies. Their common enemy remained the Church of England and its heavy-handed, persecuting bishops. Massachusetts was not fully persuaded, however, for even as Williams was en route, the General Court passed a harsh law against all Baptists, or "Anabaptists," charging them with being "incendiaries of commonwealths & the infectors of persons in main matters of religion." Anyone opposing infant baptism or persuading others to oppose it, together with anyone resisting the civil magistrate's rule in matters of religion, "shall be sentenced to banishment."

But Massachusetts, under pressure from Parliament, did allow Williams to make his way safely, without arrest or interference, from Boston to his own colony. With those who accompanied him from London, Williams set out on foot on the 40-mile trek to Providence—but this time not through winter snows. As he and his party drew nearer to his home, many prepared to give him a rousing welcome as canoes crowded around to assist him across the Seekonk River. This September was made even more joyful because he could for the first time greet another son, born during his stay in London. The family reunion had only a few weeks for celebration, however, because in November, Williams, now in his early forties, was elected "chief officer" of the newly chartered colony.

The duties of a chief officer ranged from the petty to the substantial. Governing a small colony resembled in many respects the kinds of duties assumed in that period by a town council or even a neighborhood association. One of the problems that Williams faced quite early was wolves: how to control them or get rid of them. On Aquidneck Island, some Narraganset Indians were hired to destroy the wolves, with a bounty to be paid them or any English hunter who brought in "any of the wolves' heads that are upon the Island." In Providence, Williams urged the town to find "some speedy course of [payment] for killing a wolf." New settlers had little hope of building up their flocks of sheep or herds of cattle as long as wolves freely roamed and ferociously attacked.

Then, more humanely, Roger Williams expressed his concern for the needy, the widowed, the orphaned, the unmarried, and the mentally ill in his colony. In a letter to the town fathers (January 22, 1651), Williams urged that a certain Widow Smith be dealt with fairly. Her husband, John, had operated a grist mill (for grinding grain) for the

Very little of Roger Williams's personal property has survived, but this sundial and compass are thought to be his. Of English manufacture, they date from around the middle of the 17th century.

whole town. Now, in his absence, the widow and her son needed some of the product of the mill to survive. How much should belong to the town, and how much to the family? The tensions grew to the point that Williams begged the town to "study how to put an end to that controversy." The deceased John Smith should not haunt them from his grave; rather, Williams said, we have the opportunity to show to all around us "that Providence is not only a wise but a grateful people to the God of mercies, and all his instruments of mercy toward us."

One of the town's leading citizens had died in 1647, leaving an unmarried daughter to fend for herself. When Williams learned that the daughter was about to accept a proposal of marriage, with no father to advise or look out for her, he called upon the town for its "fatherly care, counsel, and direction" on behalf of the "poor maid." Williams had some doubts about the reliability and fidelity of the young man in question, which made it all the more urgent for the town to oversee the marriage, if it in fact were to take place; otherwise, "a just reproof and charges [will] befall ourselves."

In a day when no agencies existed to look after the poor or orphaned or widowed, the town had no choice, Williams felt, but to assume the role of protector. Another widow, mentally unstable, or as Williams put it, "a distracted woman," could no longer manage her own affairs. "My request," he wrote the town fathers, "is that you would be pleased to take what is left of hers into your own hand and appoint some to order it for her supply." This again was what a merciful and generous town must do, a town "that hath received many mercies from Heaven." We should also remember, Williams added, that many of us may leave widows or orphans behind ourselves, or be deprived of our reason, and it would be good to have a precedent established for implementing the town's loving care.

Many other practical matters pressed themselves upon the government as well: building bridges, handling lawsuits for injury to animals or property, laying out boundaries for new towns or settling old claims, erecting garrisons or forts for protection against Indian attacks, determining the conditions for voting, and settling numerous disputes among neighbors. Sometimes the disputes became personal. For example, William Coddington, a resident of Portsmouth, had assumed authority over all Aquidneck Island by the time Williams obtained his precious charter. Protective of his own authority and convinced that the "islanders" (in Portsmouth and Newport) had little in common with the "mainlanders" (in Providence and Warwick), Coddington pushed for a division that would recognize his authority alone on Aquidneck.

Williams saw this as a serious threat to the infant colony, a major challenge to its charter, and a personal attack upon himself. In August 1648, he wondered how he might bring water and not "oil or fuel to the flame." Rhode Island, he was convinced, had to take charge of its own house, had to solve its own problems. It could not appeal to Massachusetts or Connecticut to help, for these neighbors would seize the opportunity to divide Rhode Island between them. Nor could it could appeal to England, for that would endanger the charter so recently granted. And, worst of all, it could not settle the matter by force, for a resort to "arms and swords is cruel and merciless." Rhode

Island's problems, Williams argued, must be settled by Rhode Islanders.

So Williams proposed that 10 men be appointed from each of the four towns, creating a grand committee of arbitration "to examine every public difference, grievance, and obstruction of justice, peace, and common safety." Within a month, it was clear that this visionary effort would produce no unanimous results. Coddington, meanwhile, attempted to make an alliance with Plymouth Colony to "adopt" his island, or place it under its civil protection. Williams managed to stop that effort by explaining to his Plymouth friends that Coddington spoke only for himself or, at most, for a pitiful few in Portsmouth. Besides, such an action would violate the 1644 charter.

The charter! Coddington was sick of Williams and his priceless charter. He would go to England himself and get his own charter. Then let Williams or the "mainlanders" do what they could about that. Early in 1649, Coddington did sail for London to carry on his plots and schemes there. By the summer of 1651 he was back in Portsmouth, which was bad enough news all by itself. But the news grew worse: he had in fact received his charter. Appearing before the Council of State in London, he had argued that he was the sole discoverer of Aquidneck Island and its sole owner, having purchased the entire acreage from the Indians. After a year of deliberation and a total failure to contact Roger Williams, the Council granted Coddington his request and appointed him governor for life.

This was a terrible blow to Williams, and potentially to the colony as a whole. Those opposed to Coddington and his unrestrained political ambitions realized that some counterforce was immediately required. And that force had to be felt in London. So, perhaps, two respected leaders could make the case against Coddington: John Clarke from Newport, on behalf of the islanders loyal to Williams, and, of course, Williams himself on behalf of the mainlanders who wanted to keep Rhode Island as one colony, not two. Pressure mounted for the two men to make the difficult voyage to save the troubled land.

But Roger Williams was most reluctant to go. For one thing, it had taken years for the towns to compensate him for the 1643–44 stay in London when he spent much of his time on colony business. Slowly the promised payments began to trickle in, but by 1650—six years after his return—the debt had not yet been fully paid. Further, he now had a large family of four sons, two daughters, and a wife who depended upon him, and he desired above all to protect and provide for them. He was also struggling to reach some kind of financial stability. He still had his Indian trading post south of Providence; he raised goats on a small island in Narragansett Bay; he was contemplating helping Providence to establish an ironworks somewhere in the town. Could he leave all that until he returned from another long trip to London?

On the other hand, no one cared more deeply about preserving Rhode Island's security and independence than he. Also, no one resented more keenly the efforts of William Coddington to divide the colony and cancel its charter. Many settlers, concerned about the security of their own properties, urged him to make this additional sacrifice. In October 1651, he wrote to his Connecticut friend, John Winthrop, Jr., that "my neighbors of Providence and Warwick...with importunities have overcome me to endeavor the renewing of their liberties upon the occasion of Mr. Coddington's late grant." Having yielded to their urgent pleas, he sold his trading post and other properties as he prepared to depart from—where? Would it be the more convenient Boston or the more distant New Amsterdam?

Swallowing his pride, Williams sat down to write a polite letter to the General Court of Massachusetts Bay, asking that he be permitted to cross over into their territory for the sole purpose of taking a ship to London. He reminded the authorities that since his banishment (which had caused him "bitter afflictions and miseries, losses, sorrows, and hardships"), he had been a model citizen. He had rendered great service not merely to Rhode Island but to all of New England in peace and in war. "Scarce a week hath passed but some way or other I have been used as instrumental to the peace and spreading of the English plantings in this country." But if any should think that he sought permission to enter Massachusetts in order to cause trouble or

When Roger Williams was a boy in late 17th-century London, the city, its skyline jagged with churches, was well on its way to becoming England's dominant metropolis.

create controversy, he "humbly" prayed that he would find only courtesy and civility in the Bay Colony, and he would render the same. He would go directly to his ship, "inoffensively behaving myself." After due deliberation, the General Court decided that Roger Williams could embark from Boston, "provided he carry himself inoffensively according to his promise."

In November 1651, Roger Williams of Providence and John Clarke of Newport sailed for London. These two able, university-educated leaders could move with ease in the higher levels of London's political circles, as they desperately needed to do. Nothing could be accomplished on behalf of Rhode Island without influential friends, without the ability to reach the ears of the members of Parliament who held the fate of the colony in their hands. Williams renewed his contacts with Oliver Cromwell and extended his friendship with John Milton, now appointed Secretary of Foreign Tongues. (Williams helped Milton learn Dutch.) He turned over additional manuscripts to a London printer and shared confidences with Sir Henry Vane regarding affairs back in New England. He wrote encouraging letters back to Providence and after several months in London was able to report one terrific bit of good news. On October 2, 1652, the Council of State had in effect cancelled Coddington's charter and instructed Providence Plantations to assume direction of the whole colony until further notice.

Williams's charter of 1644 had not yet been officially reconfirmed, but Coddington's had been officially set aside. This would do for the time, until the Council gave its "further notice" regarding the charter. How long that would take no one knew. But by the fall of 1652, Williams recognized that such action would not come quickly. The English were distracted by war with Holland, and Parliament was distracted by Cromwell's threats to disband that body. Williams wrote to his friend and printer back in Providence, Gregory Dexter, that "I see now the mind of the Lord to hold me here one year longer." The settling of all affairs and controversies pertaining to Rhode Island will be, said Williams, "a work of time."

But time hung heavy on a man who wrote early in 1653 to the towns of Warwick and Providence, which he represented, "Remember, I am a father and a husband." Earlier, he confessed to Dexter that he had been writing to his wife about the possibility of her and the family joining him in London. "I tell her how joyful I should be of her being here with me until our affairs were ended." But then, "I consider our many children, the danger of the seas, and enemies...." So, Williams concluded, he would leave the decision up to his wife whether to come or stay, "according as she finds her spirit free and cheerful." Mary Williams never found her spirit sufficiently cheerful to make that long, dangerous voyage.

Williams's spirit was not very cheerful, either. He expected to get paid for his services to the colony, especially since that had been the promise upon which he agreed to come. But early in 1653 the citizens of Providence and Warwick wrote apologetically that because of internal "distractions we cannot at present supply you with money as we ought." They would endeavor, however, to look after Williams's large family in his absence. Williams, though grateful to the towns in their concern for his family, longed to return home, but, he wrote, "I have not been willing to withdraw my shoulders from the burden lest it pinch others, and may fall heavily upon all." He would stay at his post.

Yet when he kept hearing more and more about divisions and "distractions" back home, he began to question whether his service in London was as necessary as his service on the "mainland." By March 1654 he resolved to leave, carrying with him a letter from Oliver Cromwell that would instruct the Bay Colony to allow him, once more, to land in Boston and make his way from there to Providence. He did not need to assure the General Court that he would not linger in Massachusetts or cause any trouble there. After more than two years away from his family, the pull from that direction was strong enough to make his march to Providence as straight and as fast as possible. His family needed him, and his colony needed him.

How desperately the colony needed him was demonstrated by the residents' unending bickering and contending with each other. They seemingly did nothing but complain, even against Williams himself. He had had enough. If anyone had a right to complain, he pointed out, he certainly did. Since setting the "first English foot into these wild parts" in 1636, he had done nothing but work tirelessly and selflessly on behalf of Rhode Island. He had done the very same in London. And what had been the fruits of his labors? Nothing but grief and sorrow and bitterness.

"I have been charged with folly for that freedom and liberty which I have always stood for," he wrote. He had been blamed for every land disagreement or dispute, even though he never kept "to myself a foot of land or an inch of voice in any matter." Further, "It has been told me that I have labored for a licentious and contentious people," and Williams was often inclined to agree. One party had even called him a traitor against England, to the degree that, as he said, "I am as good as banished" by his very own people, some of whom said that they wished "I might never have landed" here. Complaints? You want to hear complaints?, cried Williams. Then listen. Who was inconveniently drawn away "from my employment and sent so vast a distance from my family, to do your work, of a costly and high nature, for so many days and weeks and months together, and there left to starve or steal, or beg or borrow?" You people, wrote Williams in desperation and despair, have forgotten all that you ever once knew about humility and love.

This was as harsh and bitter a letter as Williams ever wrote to his fellow citizens of Providence. And how did they respond? They elected him President of Providence Plantations. He served in that capacity from 1654 to 1657, when he at last retired from public office, though he never lost his interest in his worrisome colony or its contentious people.

Meanwhile, what about the charter? When Williams left London in 1654, he left John Clarke behind to continue laboring on behalf of both of them to have the old charter reaffirmed or a new one granted. Neither man could have suspected that it would take Clarke nearly another 10 years to win a permanent charter for Rhode Island. Amid the many complications that Clarke confronted was England's move to restore its monarchy in 1660. If Rhode Island was to secure a solid foundation on which to build, it needed a *royal* charter: a charter issued by the king, proclaimed by the king, and guaranteed by the king.

The charter, when it finally came from the hands of King Charles II on July 8, 1663, was everything that Clarke and Williams could have hoped for. It established the boundaries for which Clarke had lobbied, begged, and prayed. It affirmed that the colony of "Rhode Island and Providence Plantations" was indeed one, not to be forever divided between the "islanders" and the "mainlanders." And, to the amazement of many—then and now—it asserted in the clearest voice that "a most flourishing civil state may stand and best be maintained...with a full liberty in religious concernments."

A "full liberty" in religion—Roger Williams had been fighting for that for more than 30 years. At this point in 1663, his fight, for the moment, seemed worth it all.

On Civic Responsibility

After laboring in London for 12 years to win a royal charter for Rhode Island (1663), John Clarke returned to Newport to put his badly neglected personal affairs back in order. Because he had not been paid for all his years of service to the colony, the General Assembly ordered a special tax on all the towns to compensate him. The town of Warwick refused to pay its share (about 80 English pounds). Much disturbed, Roger Williams wrote a strong letter to Warwick, a portion of which follows.

Providence, 1 January, 1666

Beloved Friends and Countrymen,

My due respects presented with hearty desires of your present and eternal prosperity when this short life is over. I was resolved to have visited you myself this winter, and to have persuaded you with arguments of trust and love the finishing of the payments relating to His Majesty's royal grant and charter to us. But it pleased God to visit me with old pains and lamenesses, so that sometimes I have not been able to rise, or go, or stand.

I pray your courteous leave, therefore, of saluting you with these few lines, and your favorable attention to them.

On two hinges, my discourse shall turn: first, the fairness and equity of the matter; and, second, the damage and hazard, if not performed.

As to the first, the fairness of the matter.... The first is common honesty and common justice in common dealings between man and man. This gives to every man his due: a pennyworth for a penny [spent], and will cry shame upon us that Mr. Clarke should be undone, yea, destroyed and ruined (as to this world) for his so great and so long pains, faithfulness, and diligence. He ought, in common justice, to be faithfully satisfied and honorably rewarded [even if] it had pleased God to have granted him no success, no charter, no favor in the eyes of our sovereign lord, the King.

[Even the Indians], when they send forth a public messenger, they furnish him out, they defray all payments, they gratify him with rewards. And, if he prove lame or sick and not able to return, they visit him and bring him home upon their shoulders (and that many scores of miles) with all care and tenderness.... Give me leave, therefore, to maintain my second part of the hinge, which is the hazard we run by not freely discharging [our debt]. We have only three choices. Either Mr. Clarke must patiently lie in the pit, and languish and perish (I speak as to us, for I know there is a Paymaster in the heavens who will not fail him). Or, second, some volunteers must patiently put under their shoulders and bear the common burden which, for myself, I am ready to do, although I part with the clothes from my back. Or, third, the [tax] must be taken by [force] in the King's name and authority, and this, we know, will be more grievous and more [expensive]....

If we wholly neglect this business, what will become of our credit? Will not our stink reach the nostrils of our neighbors, yea, of all inhabitants of the world that hear of us?... Again, who knows what storms and tempests [await] us? Who now will ever by employed by such masters, in whatever [difficulties] we may come into? Hath not God taught beasts and bird to be shy of being deceived, especially the second time?...

Worthy friends, the changes of the heavens and the earth have been great and sudden, seen and felt by us all this winter. Let us not soothe and sing ourselves to sleep with murderous lullabies. Let us provide for changes and, by timely humiliation, prevent them. For myself, seeing what I see all over New England, I cannot but say with David (Psalm 119), "My flesh trembleth for thee, and I am afraid of thy judgments."

Lord open the King of englāds eies.

For English-speaking Protestants of the 17th century, the most widely read book other than the Bible was John Foxe's Book of Martyrs, from which this engraving of an execution is drawn. The book ensured that England's religious persecutions would be burned in the memories of later generations.

THE CHAMPION OF RELIGIOUS LIBERTY

When Roger Williams arrived in London in 1643, he had three major matters on his mind. First, he wanted to find a wider audience for his observations of the Native Americans. Second, he was determined to gain some kind of legal recognition for his colony. And third, he desired to make the case, as strongly and as passionately as possible, on behalf of religious freedom. This was the driving force for Williams for a half-century or more. That passion, more than any other single facet of Williams's life, is responsible for the monuments that have been raised in his honor: from Geneva, Switzerland, to Washington, D.C., to Bristol and Providence, Rhode Island.

Americans in the 21st century may have some difficulty accepting the idea that one had to fight, valiantly and fearlessly, for religious liberty. Does not everyone believe in religious liberty? That we can even raise such a question is a tribute to the labors, three and a half centuries ago, of Roger Williams. For in the 17th century, the answer to such a question would have been an emphatic "No!" Indeed, at that time hardly anyone believed in religious liberty. And not only did they not believe in it, they were horrified by the prospect of it. The common assumption was that if religious liberty prevailed, churches would close, governments would fall and all moral standards would collapse.

Roger Williams heard those arguments—stated more like self-evident truths, really—over and over. The devil, said Massachusetts Bay historian and Williams contemporary Nathaniel Ward, would like nothing better than to see religious liberty prevail everywhere. A multiplicity of religions would lead to a worldwide loss of faith. Williams spoke often of liberty of conscience. Well, said Ward, let me tell you what true liberty of conscience is. It is the liberty "to contend earnestly for the truth; to preserve unity of spirit, faith, ordinances, to be all like minded, of one accord." For Ward, liberty meant conformity. If pushed further than that, Ward said that Williams and all other fanatics or enthusiasts like him had a perfect liberty: "a free liberty to keep away from us."

Others living in Massachusetts when Williams was banished felt obliged to point out how right the Bay Colony had been to act as it had, how wrong and how dangerous it would be to follow the perilous path that Williams walked. Their condemnation could be theoretical; it could also be personal. William Hubbard, the pastor in Ipswich, observed that all thoughtful persons, both in old England and New, agreed that Williams was conceited and uncharitable. And in the Plymouth Colony, historian Nathaniel Morton declared concerning the "great and lamentable apostacy" of Williams that citizens in general needed to be warned about the dangers of "forsaking the churches of Christ and ordinances of God among them."

Almost a century later, Massachusetts was still doing its best to purge the poison of Roger Williams from its system. The Reverend Cotton Mather of Boston, noted theologian and author in 1702 of a religious history of New England, told a story that nicely conveyed his impression of Roger Williams. Mather had heard of a windmill in Holland that in 1654 was whipped by such high winds that the revolving millstones grew too hot and set first the mill on fire, then the whole town. "But I can tell my readers that, about twenty years before this, there was a whole country in America like to be set on fire by the rapid motion of a windmill in the head of one particular man." The man, of course, was Roger Williams, who had "less light than fire in him." Fortunately, the Bay Colony managed to put out the fire, Mather happily noted, by banishing Williams from its midst. To have allowed him to continue spreading his delusions and fiery opinions would have turned all Massachusetts into a "sink of abominations."

Thus, the 17th century did not look kindly upon religious liberty, nor upon those lonely few who advocated it. Williams could talk about it, write letters about it, but could not in New England get anything published about it. The consensus there was that dangerous opinions deserved to be suppressed, not spread all around like wildfire. Williams exchanged letters with John Cotton, his chief adversary in Boston, but most of this correspondence has

Cotton Mather, Congregational pastor in Boston, prolific author, and vigorous defender of Calvinist orthodoxy, had little use for Roger Williams and even less for what Mather called his "scandalous" colony of Rhode Island.

been lost. Williams would, however, put the essentials of his controversy with Cotton in book form and search in London for a printer who would give his views more permanence.

Before that large book emerged, however, Williams, in London, decided to address Parliament itself. After all, he was on the English scene at a critical juncture, with civil war under way, Parliament forging an alliance with Scotland to help defeat the forces of King Charles I, Oliver Cromwell filling the power vacuum with his leadership and his army, and some members of Parliament trying to find a middle path between the Presbyterianism of Scotland and the bursting forth of new religions that threatened to flood all England. Those searching for a middle way had written a small tract posing the problem as they saw it. As Williams saw it, however, the far greater problem was their reluctance to embrace a full religious liberty.

So he responded with a 20-page tract called "Queries of Highest Consideration": that is, questions that in those difficult days in England's history demanded answers, courageous answers. One did not take on Parliament or any of its members lightly, for they held most of the power and had been thrown on the defensive by attacks from many sides. Williams decided to publish his small work anonymously because, he noted, people in power are seldom willing to "hear any other music but what is known to please them." And his answers, if not his questions, would not be all that pleasing.

Parliament had invited an assembly of clergymen from England and Scotland to advise it on religious matters. This Westminster Assembly, consisting of more than 100 clergy together with civil representatives from Scotland and Parliament's own House of Commons, held the first of its 1,200 meetings in July 1643. Williams first asked what New Testament basis could be found for such a gathering. He had himself searched the scriptures carefully and could find no precedent for this sort of "assembly of divines." Rather, he found only the local churches, only a gathering of the faithful, who exercised no civil power whatsoever. Nor, while he was busy examining his New Testament, did he find anything that looked like a pope or a king who set himself down "in the pope's chair in England" as King Henry VIII and all his successors had done. Religion was local, not national; the church was spiritual, not political, he argued.

But, some might respond, what about the Old Testament? There, surely, one could find spiritual and political power mixed together. Yes, Williams agreed, that was true. But the coming of Christ created a *new* covenant, a *new* testament, that displaced the old order found in the nation of Israel. It was time, said Williams, for England to decide whether it wanted to follow Moses or Christ. If it chose to follow Christ, then it could not find in his words or deeds the least "footstep" that would lead to the notion of a national church. If the scriptures so inform us, reason does as well. For reason reveals the absurdity of expecting one faith to fit all, which is as absurd as expecting one shoe size to fit all. As far as creating a national religion was concerned, "it seems not possible," Williams concluded, "to fit it to every conscience."

Of course, Parliament was not trying to fit the religion it chose to every conscience. Rather, it was trying to determine what was best for all England, and then it would simply direct each conscience to conform. But the Bible was full of ambiguities or "mysteries," as Williams called them. How could one hope to solve every uncertainty with such clarity and assurance as to say this was not only true for those of us in Parliament but must now be true for every citizen? We English have been through this, over and over, Williams pointed out. In the time of King Henry VIII, everyone had to cease, immediately, being a Roman Catholic and conform to the newly created Church of England. Otherwise fines, jails, whips, or swords would swiftly follow. Then, in the time of Henry's successor, Edward VI, one had to become a consistent Calvinist or suffer the scourge of the state. Then Mary I came to the throne and demanded that the kingdom become Catholic again, or endure severe penalties. And so it has continued through Elizabeth I, James I, Charles I—and now Parliament. When would this absurdity end?

Thus, Williams put another hard question to the members of Parliament. "We query whether the blood of so many hundred thousand Protestants, mingled with the blood of so many thousand papists" spilled since the Reformation "be not a warning to us." The continent of Europe had now for a hundred years been washed with the blood of people dying for their faith, of consciences subjected to a "spiritual rape." England had up to now followed that same bloody path. Was it not time to bring all this to a merciful halt? Parliament could take that blessed step, if only it would.

Williams concluded his tract with a summary of hard-hitting assertions, so no one could miss the point. First, the ancient nation of Israel was not a pattern for any modern nation, because the shadows of Moses "vanished at the coming of the Lord Jesus." Second, religious persecution was an utter violation of the Christian spirit and of fundamental humanity. Third, a national conformity required even of Jews hinders their possible conversion, because it does not grant them even the privilege of "a civil life." Fourth, religious warfare has been the curse of civilization in that it, more than any other single cause, has been responsible for the murder of countless men, women, and children. Fifth, when persons are forced to conform to a mode of worship that their "hearts embrace not," then they have been violated in the very depths of their being. And finally, anyone who says that he seeks more spiritual light but is still willing to persecute, even while seeking, scorns every standard of both Christianity and humanity.

Parliament was not persuaded. It passed strict rules for the observance of Sunday, with no games or sports, no trade or travel. It required even greater conformity in worship and belief in order to prevent, in its words, a plague of "erroneous opinions, ruinating schisms, and damnable heresies" from infecting all England. Preaching, like printing, would be allowed only under a license from the state. Individual congregations were not at liberty to follow any form of worship they might choose. Considering all this, Williams feared that a Parliamentary tyranny, no more pleasing than a kingly tyranny, would like a dark cloud spread all across his native land.

But he had another land to worry about as well.

THE FOLLY AND CRUELTY OF RELIGIOUS PERSECUTION

In The Bloudy Tenent of Persecution, for Cause of Conscience. A Conference between Truth and Peace, presented to the High Court of Parliment, in all Tender Affection, amongst other Passages of Highest Consideration *(1644); Roger Williams poured out his fury at the absurdity, the inhumanity, of fining, jailing, whipping, or killing men, women, and children for their religious beliefs. All the sword can do, he pointed out, is create hypocrites and enemies of Christianity; it has never, it can never, produce one sincere Christian. (Or, as Thomas Jefferson later wrote, the only effect of state-enforced religion was to make one half of the world fools, the other half hypocrites.)*

What a most woeful proof hereof have the nations of the earth given in all ages! And to seek no further than our native soil [England], within a few scores of years, how many wonderful changes in religion hath the whole kingdom made, according to the governors thereof:...Henry VII finds and leaves the kingdom absolutely Popish. Henry VIII casts it into a mold half Popish, half Protestant. Edward VI brings forth an edition all Protestant. Queen Mary, within a few years, defaces Edward's work, and renders the kingdom (after the pattern of her grandfather, Henry VII) all Popish. Mary's short life and religion end together. Elizabeth revives the model of her brother, Edward: all Protestant....

It hath been England's sinful shame to fashion and change her garments and religions with wondrous ease and lightness, as a higher power, a stronger sword, hath prevailed. This follows the ancient pattern of Nebuchadnezzar bowing the whole world in one most solemn uniformity of worship in his golden image (Daniel 3).

Beyond the Atlantic Ocean, Williams had confronted a Bay Colony tyranny face to face and in 1635 had lost his battle against it. Now, almost a decade later, he was ready to engage the battle again—not with physical swords or guns, to be sure, but with the spiritual weapons of persuasion and love. With his Bible by his side and his banishment never far from his mind, he would challenge John Cotton of Boston to come out of his study and fight. When Williams had assembled all his spiritual artillery in publishable form, he called it (the 17th century believed in long titles) *The Bloudy Tenent of Persecution, for Cause of Conscience. A Conference between Truth and Peace, presented to the High Court of Parliament, in all Tender Affection, amongst other Passages of Highest Consideration.*

Understandably referred to simply as *The Bloudy Tenent,* this long and somewhat disorganized book labored to get at the essence of the argument between Williams and Cotton, between Rhode Island and Massachusetts, between liberty and conformity in matters of religion. Williams called persecution "bloudy" (that is, bloody) in at least two senses: first, its practice managed to spill much blood across many lands; second, as a kind of slang, "bloudy" expressed contempt for and condemnation of whatever followed. A tenent (what modern English calls "tenet") refers to a doctrine or principle that one holds to be true. So a good part of the message of Roger Williams in his 1644 book is contained in the title: the forcing of any person's conscience, against her or his will, is a totally evil deed; moreover, that compulsion was responsible for oceans of innocent blood staining the whole earth.

In all that followed his long title, Williams concentrated on four key issues: whether Massachusetts had dealt with him fairly, whether the Bay Colony churches knew a pure form of worship, whether religious liberty ought to prevail, and how church and state should relate to each other. That was a large order, even for a large book.

THE
BLOVDY TENENT,
of PERSECUTION, for caufe of
CONSCIENCE, difcuffed, in

A Conference betweene
TRVTH and PEACE.

VVHO,

In all tender Affection, prefent to the High
Court of *Parliament,* (as the *Refult* of
their *Difcourfe*) thefe, (amongft other
Paffages) of *higheft confideration.*

Printed in the Year 1644.

This is Roger Williams's most famous—or infamous—book, burned in London soon after it was published in 1644 and despised in Massachusetts for decades afterward.

First was the banishment, which continued to fester like a sore in Williams's memory. He could understand being ejected from his church if he proposed doctrines with which its members could not agree. But to have his very citizenship taken from him, his right to live and work and feed his family, struck Williams as far more than justice required. He had not been violent, he had not advocated rebellion or revolution, he had not stormed the halls or homes of those in power. Yet, "without mercy and human compassion," he had been driven into the "miseries" of a wintry wilderness, there to perish, so far as anyone in the Bay Colony knew or cared. Clearly, he had been mistreated and abused but now, in 1644, even larger issues were at stake.

How true or pure was the church that Massachusetts had created, and now defended at the point of a sword? Not very pure, not very true, in Williams's strong opinion. In theory, New England made the magistrate supreme in civil affairs, the church supreme in spiritual affairs. There was nothing wrong with that theory, Williams granted. But in practice, the Bay Colony made the magistrate the enforcer of religious duties and doctrines. Here was the absurdity. The governor was at the same time to "sit on the bench, and stand at the bar of Christ Jesus." In effect, the civil magistrate had been made the absolute head of the church as much as Henry VIII or Charles I had been the head of the Church of England. If the colony's officers were the protectors of true doctrine and the punishers of heretics, "what is this in true plain English" but to make them the judges of *all* truth, civil or spiritual?

If the state could compel a person to go to church, why stop there? Compel them also to join in the Lord's Supper, or—even more ridiculous—compel them to be converted. If persons are forced to adopt a particular religion, the end result, said Williams, was that they would in their hearts "be of no religion at all, all their days." In this matter, as in all others, one should take the New Testament as an all-sufficient guide. Consider that when the apostle Paul entered the city of Corinth, he did not go to the city's magistrate to urge him to compel people to listen to what he had to say. Maybe that was because Paul did not fully understand what the New England model of a "true church" really was!

This argument led easily to Williams's third point: religious toleration. It should be noted immediately that "toleration" was not the word that Williams would have used, for toleration implied some kind of concession by a ruler or a bishop who had the sacred right to persecute but on some occasions graciously chose not to. This was all wrong, Williams insisted. Liberty in religion was a God-given right that no bishop or king or state or colony could rightfully deny. So Williams argued for, fought for, religious freedom, or as he often said, "soul liberty." This belonged to all human beings by virtue of their humanity—as much as their right to breathe, as much their right as life itself, they had the right in religion to be wholly free.

In his foreword to *The Bloudy Tenent* Williams explained that this liberty must not be restricted to Protestants or even to all Christians. It must be without bounds or limits, protective of all tender consciences everywhere: "paganish, Jewish, Turkish, or anti-christian." Those who proposed religious toleration (as opposed to religious freedom) generally limited that toleration quite strictly. This was true, for example, of England's Act of Toleration, passed a half-century after this book by Williams appeared. That act eased the door open wide enough to include most Protestants, but none who denied the doctrine of the Trinity, nor any who accepted the authority of the pope, and certainly not any who were pagans, Muslims, Jews, or enemies of the Christian religion. No wonder that the notion of toleration held little appeal for Roger Williams.

In his book's preface, addressed to the "Courteous Reader," Williams asked such a reader to consider what Jesus would do were he in London in 1644. Which religion would he endorse? "Mine," everyone confidently replied. All right, said Williams, I do not want to argue about that. But my next question is this: What weapons would he provide to see that the religion which Parliament endorsed was followed by all in England? And the answer to that was clear: none. Just as he employed no weapons in his own ministry except those of persuasion and love, so were only those instruments available to his faithful followers. England had taken steps, Williams happily noted, to see that the

Bible was widely available, even "to the poorest English houses," in the language of the people. But how ironic, how tragic, that the kingdom would not then allow people to reach their own religious convictions on the basis of reading their own Bibles. One might as well live in Spain or Rome, Williams noted, where no one pretends that the conscience should be free.

Here in England, he observed, we make church membership (of course, in the Church of England only) a condition for voting, for holding office, for attending the universities. We are asked to trade our religion for political favor, for social standing, for public approval. But this was not the way of the cross, nor should it be our way. "Having bought truth dear," Williams wrote, "we must not sell it cheap, not the least grain of it for the whole world."

That attitude might result in persecution. So be it. That attitude might lead to martydom or death by burning or hanging. So be it. After all, Christ set the example here as well. If one wished only to compromise, to accommodate, to do the nice and polite thing, then one should look elsewhere for religious allegiance or affiliation—not to Christianity. The sanctuary of the soul should never be invaded by sheriffs or jailers, by judges or soldiers. That sanctuary was, is, and will ever be God's own sacred place, reserved to him alone. Now, in 1644, Parliament must beware that it does not do violence to those sacred consciences. May it never be said "that the Parliament of England hath committed a greater rape, than if they had forced or ravished the bodies of all the women in the world." Because Williams felt strongly about religious liberty and the sanctity of conscience, his language grew strong as well.

To put it simply, the Christian church does not persecute. Therefore, the church that persecutes is not Christian. For religious persecution contradicts "the spirit and mind and practice of the Prince of peace." Beyond that, however, persecution has destroyed and continues to destroy the civil peace of kingdoms, countries, and commonwealths every-where. Christ is not delighted with the shedding of the blood of others, Williams pointed out, but "shed his own for his bloodiest enemies."

It was now time, if not past time, declared Williams, for the civil sword to be put back into its sheath. If England could do that then it would have a second "Magna Carta of highest liberties," stated Williams, referring to the basic charter of English liberties from the 13th century. If England could do that, then every humble cottage in the land, reveling in a new security and new freedom, could decorate its front doors with olive branches, the symbol of peace. Then at long last, the "doleful drums, and shrill sounding trumpets, the roaring murdering canons, the shouts of conquerors, [and] the groans of wounded, dying, slaughtered righteous with the wicked" would be stilled. Here was a voice crying in the wilderness, but a voice that would not be stilled.

And so what of the proper relationship between the church and the state? Beginning with the Roman emperor, Constantine in the fourth century, the fatal habit developed of defending spiritual truths with physical force. The emperor Nero, who in the first century burned Rome and burned Christians, proved to be a better friend to true Christianity than was Constantine, for Nero did not corrupt the church by mixing religion and politics together to such an extent that one could not pry them apart. But Constantine introduced a fatal confusion into Christ's religion, said Williams, when he created this political-religious, messy mixture called Christendom. It is because of Christendom that we have come to speak of Christian nations, Christian states, Christian institutions. For Williams, there were no such things. There was only Christianity, a truth that dwells only in the hearts and souls of women and men. It is not found in kingdoms, for kingdoms do not convert, do not receive the grace of God, do not enter into heaven.

THE

BLOUDY TENENT,

WASHED,

And made white in the bloud of the
Lambe: being discussed and discharged of
bloud-guiltinesse by just Defence.

WHEREIN

The great Questions of this present time are
handled, *viz.* How farre Liberty of Conscience
ought to be given to those that truly feare God? And how farre
restrained to turbulent and pestilent persons, that not one-
ly raze the foundation of Godlinesse, but disturb the Civill
Peace where they live? Also how farre the Magistrate may proceed in the duties of the first Table? And that all Magistrates
ought to study the word and will of God, that they may frame
their Government according to it.

DISCUSSED.

As they are alledged from divers Scriptures, out of
the Old and New Testament. Wherein also the practise of
Princes is debated, together with the Judgement of Ancient and late Writers of most precious esteeme.

Whereunto is added a Reply to Mr. WILLIAMS
Answer, to Mr. COTTONS Letter.

BY JOHN COTTON Batchelor in Divinity, and
Teacher of the Church of Christ at *Boston* in *New-England.*

LONDON,
Printed by *Matthew Symmons* for *Hannah Allen*, at the *Crowne* in
Popes Head-Alley. 1 6 4 7.

So the time had come to undo what Constantine,
1,300 years before, had done. The state had its proper role
and the churches theirs. The state might assist the church
only in the sense that it maintained peace and order in the
society. The church might assist the state only in the sense
that it might "cast a blush of civility and morality" upon its
citizens. Well, some say, look at Geneva in Switzerland.
There, under the leadership of John Calvin, even Protestants

had created a solid union of church and state. He had looked at Geneva, Williams replied, and he did not like what he saw. For it implied that the ordinances of the church might "be given by Christ to any civil state, town, or city," and that, said Williams, "I confidently deny." We must not allow ourselves to get hung up on John Calvin, he argued, any more than on Moses. The new Israel is a *spiritual* community only; the old Israel has passed away, to be replaced not by a nation but by a church. How long will it take for kings and bishops, for governors and magistrates to get this message? They have now had some 1,600 years; that should have been long enough for Christ's words to sink in: "My Kingdom is not of this world."

Of course, Williams admitted, a Christian must obey his ruler in civil matters, but in civil matters only. In religious matters, the Christian may judge his ruler as he would any other person. For example, said Williams, consider the case of a physician who must in general obey his prince. But the prince must obey the physician's prescription for the ruler's health. Magistrates cannot put themselves above other Christians in the practice of their art (that is, religion), just as princes cannot put themselves above physicians in the practice of their art (that is, medicine). This should be perfectly clear, perfectly simple to all, Williams believed. For to act in any other way was "to turn the world upside down." Then the garden of the church became indistinguishable from the weeds of the world. Religion could no longer be separated from politics, and Christ, the good shepherd, could no longer keep the wolves away from his sheep.

Roger Williams had hoped to convince Parliament to embrace religious liberty and the separation of the church from the state. He did not succeed. His book was published in July 1644; in August, Parliament ordered that it be burned. By this time, Williams was aboard a ship bound for America, carrying with him enough copies of *The Bloudy Tenent* to ensure that it would not be forgotten or ignored.

John Cotton, for one, did not ignore it. In 1647 he responded to Williams with his own book: *The Bloudy Tenent, Washed and Made White in the Bloud of the Lamb.* Cotton and Williams had, like two skilled fencers, been dueling for more than 10 years. Each knew the moves of the other, the weak points in the armor of the other. Each professed respect for the other person, even though over the years the attacks became harsher and more bitter. Each had his protective shield—whether scripture, or reason, or experience—and would not under any circumstances set it aside.

On the matter of Williams's banishment, Cotton explained that he himself had had no direct role to play in that. Then, in the manner of a parent instructing a difficult and stubborn child, Cotton tried to make clear that Williams had really banished himself. He had refused to be instructed or enlightened, refused to admit his errors and "corrupt doctrines." "You overheated yourself in reasoning and disputing," Cotton explained. You found errors and failings in everyone else, "rather than in yourself." In fact, Cotton added, because you could not get along with anybody in the Bay Colony, "I would think it a work of mercy of God to banish me from the civil society of such a commonwealth, when I could not enjoy the holy fellowship of any." Don't blame us, Roger Williams; blame yourself.

On the purity of the Massachusetts churches, Cotton took this issue so seriously that he wrote extensively on that subject, both in this book and others to come. The Puritans' churches were not really pure, Williams had argued, but Cotton replied that Williams demanded a level of purity beyond the reach of mortal man. We have decried the pollutions of the national church, said Cotton, and we "humble our souls" for having formerly been part of that corrupt establishment. But "we deny that it is necessary to church fellowship" to explicitly condemn and "bewail all the pollutions" of the Church of England. All that was necessary was that members "be ready in preparation of heart, as they shall see more light, so to hate more and more every false way." Williams demanded instant transformation; we, much more realistically, said Cotton, expect a steady pilgrimage from darkness to light.

On the more central matter of religious liberty, Cotton and Williams took a parable from the New Testament and wrested from it every possible ounce of meaning. Of course, they came out on opposite sides. The parable concerned the wheat and the tares (or weeds). A farmer's enemy had deliberately planted weeds in his wheat field. The laborers were ready to rip them out, but the farmer said that would also disturb the growing wheat. So, he advised: "Let both grow together until the harvest; and in the time of harvest, I will say to the reapers, Gather ye together first the tares, and bind them in bundles to burn them, but gather the wheat into my barn" (Matthew 13:24–30). Now, Jesus said that the kingdom of heaven was like this field of wheat and tares, so just what was the message?

For Williams the message was clear: saints and sinners could live together and even worship together until God at the time of the harvest (the judgment day) made the sure separation of wheat from tares, of saints from sinners. Cotton held that the words were taken out of context and that the historical examples were arbitrarily selected. First, in all the talk about conscience, one must distinguish between a "conscience rightly informed" and an "erroneous and blind conscience." The former must be honored and listened to, but not the latter. Can anyone really believe, Cotton wonderingly asked, that a "heretic, after once or twice" being admonished, "may be tolerated either in the church without excommunication, or in the Commonwealth without such punishment as may preserve others from dangerous and damnable infection?" For Cotton, the question answered itself. Heresy was like a plague or a disease. To tolerate it, or—worse—to grant it liberty, was to invite disaster down upon the entire social order. No reasonable human being would support that. Except, of course, Roger Williams.

Williams also could not believe that the Puritans who had themselves fled from persecution in England would end up persecuting others in Massachusetts. How could John Cotton justify or explain that? Easily, said Cotton. "We believe there is a vast difference between men's inventions and God's institutions. We fled from men's inventions," he explained, but "we compel none to men's inventions." In other words, we and God are in perfect agreement; if you resist our way, you resist God's institutions.

Regarding the matter of separating church and state, again, no reasonable human being, Cotton asserted, would not grant to the magistrate the right to enforce the first four commandments, concerning loving God and not cursing him, forbidding idolatry, and preserving Sunday (or the Sabbath) as a holy day. No reasonable human being could fail to see in the Old Testament the example of a civil order giving its support and protection to the religious order.

This monument, erected in 1906, marks the spot of Roger Williams's landing in Rhode Island. The marker is dedicated "To the memory of Roger Williams, the Apostle of Soul Liberty."

Except, of course, Roger Williams, who thought that Jesus had replaced Moses and was convinced that Christianity never shined so brightly as when it was persecuted. Just as stars are brightest on the darkest nights and as spices give off their finest aromas when ground, pounded, and burned, so Christianity flourishes not in the arms of kings and princes but when it stands boldly against them—and alone.

These arguments could and did cover the same ground so often that their original paths had been destroyed. These fields of discussion had been plowed from every direction and at varying depths. Williams did not budge

Cotton, nor did Cotton dislodge Williams from his dug-in positions. With *The Bloudy Tenent* under his arm and in his heart, Williams returned to Providence.

Back in Rhode Island, Roger Williams did not have to wait long to discover that the controversy between him and Cotton was more than a matter of mere words. Religious liberty could still be denied, blood could still be shed. Down in Newport, John Clarke, along with two other members of his Baptist church, responded to the plea of a blind Baptist in Massachusetts to hold a service of worship in his home. Ever since the 1644 law against Baptists, no Baptist church could legally exist within the borders of the Bay Colony. On July 16, 1651, therefore, the three Newporters journeyed to Lynn, Massachusetts, where they preached, prayed, baptized new believers, and served communion—all in the home of the aged Baptist who had invited them.

On July 20, as John Clarke was expounding the gospel, two constables "with their clamorous tongues" interrupted the meeting and arrested the three "strangers," as Clarke later described the event. After a week or more in a Boston jail, the three were brought into court, tried in the morning, and sentenced in the afternoon, "without," said Clarke, "producing either accuser, witness, jury, law of God or man." They had been charged with "seducing the subjects of this Commonwealth from the truth of the Gospel of Jesus Christ" and with daring to baptize those who, as infants, had been baptized before. Clarke demanded the right to be heard on behalf of the three defendants, but his request was denied. All three were fined, with the stipulation that if the fines were not paid they would be "well whipped."

Eventually, during August friends paid the fines of two of the three. Only one, Obadiah Holmes, did not pay his fine, and refused to let others pay it. On September 5 he was brought to Boston's marketplace, tied to a post, and stripped to the waist to receive 30 lashes with a three-pronged whip on his bare back. Holmes responded to his persecutors, saying: "I am now come to be baptized in afflictions by your hands."

When Roger Williams heard of this event, he was enraged. Normally, when he wrote to a governor of Massachusetts, he was respectful and restrained. This time he was neither, as he addressed Governor John Endicott in

Despite his banishment from the Massachusetts Bay Colony, Roger Williams continued to correspond with its governor, John Winthrop, addressing him respectfully as "Much Honoured Sir."

the severest tones. What possible justification could the governor offer for this barbaric treatment of a fellow Christian? How is it, Williams asked, that persons speak so tenderly of their own consciences yet have "so little respect, mercy, or pity to the like conscientious persuasion of other men?" Oh, please do not tell me that this poor Baptist, Obadiah Holmes, sinned against his own conscience. I have heard all that before, and not only from John Cotton. For "that is the outcry of Pope and Prelates, and Scotch Presbyterians, who would fire all the world, to be avenged on the...blasphemous heretics, the seducing heretics" and whoever else dared to provoke them.

Governor Endicott, he wrote, please have respect for conscience, every conscience. Do "remember that that thing which we call conscience is of such a nature (especially in Englishmen) as once a pope in Rome...himself observed that although it be groundless, false, and deluded, yet it is not by any arguments or torments easily removed." Besides, how can you be so certain that you are right, and that so many millions of others are wrong? How can you be sure that in persecuting the many you do not end up persecuting Christ himself?

Listen carefully, governor. For you may hear "a dreadful voice from the King of Kings, the Lord of Lords: Endicott, Endicott, why huntest thou me? Why imprisonest thou me? Why so finest, why so bloodily whippest?" The time has come, governor, for you to face a terrifying possibility. "Is it possible...that since I hunt, I hunt not the life of my Savior, and the blood of the Lamb of God? I have fought against several sorts of consciences: is it beyond all possibility and hazard that I have not fought against God, that I have not persecuted Jesus in some of them?" What reasonable man, what sincere man, would want to take a chance like that?

The reason Williams felt so strongly about this single event was that he feared that a single drop of blood today could become a rushing river tomorrow. "Like stones once rolling down the alps, like the Indians canoes or English boats loose and adrift, where stop we until infinite mercy stop us?" A fanatical religious zeal, armed with the sword, can be terrifying. God may step in to stop it, but we, armed only with religious liberty, have the power to stop it ourselves.

A former Massachusetts magistrate, then living in England, also condemned the harsh treatment of Obadiah Holmes. He wrote to Boston's church of his sadness when he learned of "your tyranny and persecutions . . . as that you fine, whip, and imprison men for their consciences." This letter aroused John Cotton, now in the last year of his life, to one final response to all this nonsense about liberty of conscience. We tolerate many who dissent "privately and inoffensively," Cotton explained, but we have not carried toleration to the extreme that some in England seem to expect. Besides, accommodations in a Boston jail were probably better than those in a Rhode Island home. As for Obadiah Holmes himself, he had probably not been so well fed or "well clad" in years.

Williams, for his part, never tired of talking about liberty, but he had trouble getting others—even in Rhode Island—to understand exactly what this liberty meant. It did not mean the dodging of all responsibility. It did not mean the abandonment of all moral standards. It did not mean defying or condemning all authority. What, then, did it mean? The Providence fathers needed to know, Rhode Island needed to know, perhaps the world at large needed to know.

In 1655, while he was serving as president of Providence Plantations, Williams wrote a letter to his town in an attempt to articulate just what religious liberty meant. It might help, he thought, to consider the analogy of a ship at sea. The passengers aboard that ship had full liberty to worship as they pleased, or not to worship at all. "Papists, Protestants, Jews, Turks"—whoever—all were free to worship in their own fashion, and none could be compelled to

attend anyone else's worship. But on the other hand, the captain of the ship had his own characteristic liberty, too: "to command the ship's course; yea, and also to command that justice, peace, and sobriety be kept and practiced, both among the seamen and all the passengers." This was not tyranny, this was civility. The ship was like a colony or a state and, at the moment, Williams was the captain of his colony. Citizens had to pay taxes, they had to fulfill their obligations to serve in the militia, they had to obey—but in civil matters only. In religion, their liberty was complete.

Why should it be so difficult, Williams asked, to see that liberty did not mean anarchy and that citizens had duties as well as rights? Williams fervently hoped that his

This gruesome wood-cut from the Book of Martyrs *shows the burning of three women, one of whom was pregnant. Her infant bursts forth from the womb.*

105

This very early map, drawn even before the founding of Providence in 1636, gives a rough idea of first settlements in Massachusetts.

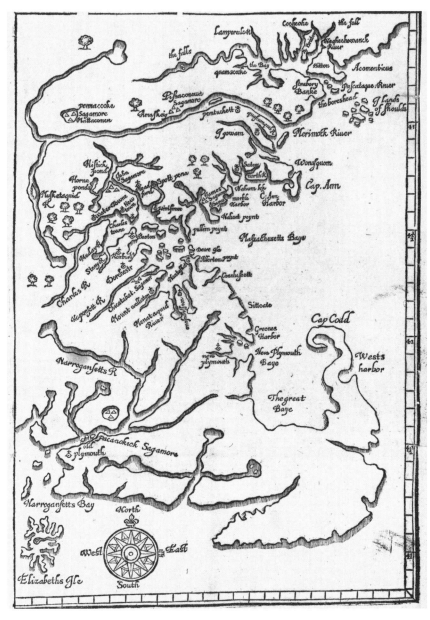

earnest communication would be enough to "let in some light, to such as willingly shut not their eyes."

Another kind of misunderstanding has historically haunted the notion of religious liberty: namely, that if one believes in religious liberty, it can only be because one is indifferent to all religion. Some people might indeed believe in religious liberty because, for them, religion matters so little. Roger Williams, on the other hand, believed in religious liberty because religion mattered so much.

In his old age, Williams rowed some 30 miles from Providence to Newport to engage the Quakers in vigorous debate, attempting to show them the error of their ways. See, some commentators say, he did not really believe in religious liberty, because he told the Quakers they were wrong! What a dreadful misunderstanding this is. Yes, Williams told the Quakers they were wrong and for several days debated their religious principles with them. But no, he did not prevent their moving to and thriving in Rhode Island. And he did not allow the hand of the state ever to be raised against them. Nor did he fine, jail, whip, or hang any Quakers, or permit others to do so. Williams, who cared deeply about his own faith and his own conscience, would, with equal passion and devotion, ever care about and protect the conscience of others.

Williams had spent so much time in the defense of religious liberty, in both old and New England, that he had often neglected his own welfare, even including that of his own family. In trying to make a living at his Indian trading post, he frequently invited members of his family in Providence to join him, thinking that the salt breezes and country air would do them good. In 1649, he grew increasingly concerned about the health of his oldest daughter, Mary, who suffered from particularly severe headaches. He tried healing herbs and native plants recommended by the Indians, but her condition grew no better. The troubled father then wrote to his old friend John Winthrop, asking about the best physicians in Boston. But Mary's condition gradually improved enough that she never had to make the trip. She later married and had a family of her own.

When abroad, Williams suffered from the long separations from his family. In 1652, he even thought of bringing his wife and children to London when obtaining a charter for Rhode Island took longer than expected. But the trip was both expensive and dangerous, and the family never joined him there.

The private correspondence of Roger Williams to members of his family has, unfortunately, not survived. One can only guess at the tender affections expressed there. A single, small, personal book remains, however, a kind of love letter to his wife, encouraging her in times of illness or depression. Called *Experiments of Spiritual Life & Health,* this work contains no controversy, only consolation. Williams presented this book to his wife as one would a bouquet on a special occasion: "This handful of flowers made up in a little posy, for thy dear self, and our dear children, to look on and smell on, when I as the grass of the field shall be gone and withered."

This statue of Roger Williams, long installed in the rotunda of the U.S. Capitol, carries his urgent message of "soul liberty."

When life seemed hard and thoughts grew dark, it was time, Williams wrote, to remember that we are on this earth, "like passengers on a ship," making our way to a heavenly home. If defeated now, we shall be victorious then; if despised and persecuted now, we shall be crowned and treated as royalty then. In short, dear wife, he urged, always remember that after our few short years of labor and suffering here, we shall someday reap a "never-ending harvest of inconceivable joys." Beyond politics and charters, away from bishops and kings, freed from all sorrows and swords, heaven awaited.

Meanwhile, the citizens of Providence continued to quarrel, to dispute, and to disobey. Wearily, an aged Roger Williams wrote to them in 1682 to remind them that government was legitimate and had a proper role to play in their contentious lives. "There is not a man in the world," he told them, "(except robbers, pirates, rebels) but doth submit to government." His friends and neighbors must choose between war and peace. The very next year, Williams chose peace, as his worn and aching body was laid to rest. The exact date of his death, like that of his birth, is unknown. No state funeral was held, no monument built, no eulogies delivered. If in later years monuments were erected, they would largely be of another kind.

By the time that Thomas Nast was penning his editorial cartoons in the late 19th century, the separation of church and state had in America become a commonplace idea. Here a figure representing American liberty raises her hand, forbidding various religious groups entry into the realm of the state.

ROGER WILLIAMS AND AMERICA

When Roger Williams was exiled from Massachusetts in 1635, John Cotton explained that Williams had not so much been banished as "enlarged" to the whole wild country beyond the Bay Colony's borders. Cotton was speaking with some sarcasm. No one, centuries later, would be more surprised than Cotton to learn that Williams has indeed been "enlarged." His influence has grown, while that of Cotton has diminished. The pleas of the Rhode Island radical for liberty of conscience spoke more for an age that would come than it did to his own time.

Even in the 17th century, one could detect small signs of movement from conformity to liberty. The 1663 royal charter of Rhode Island, for example, had spoken of Rhode Islanders having it "much on their hearts (if they be permitted) to hold forth a lively experiment." That experiment was designed to test the proposition that a civil society could actually flourish even with (possibly because of?) a full liberty in "religious concernments." Roger Williams had earlier looked to Holland as a support for his argument. The Dutch nation had flourished in shipping and trade all over the world; prospering at home, it had also enlarged its possessions abroad. And it had managed to do this while granting more religious toleration than was to be found anywhere else in Europe.

Now the time had come for New World governments to test the proposition, to launch out on their own "lively experiments." Following the lead of Rhode Island, several seemed prepared to do just that. King Charles II had in the 1663 charter laid the firm foundation:

> Our royal will and pleasure is that no person within the said colony, at any time hereafter, shall be in any wise molested, punished, disquieted, or called in question, for difference in opinion in matters of religion, [that] do not actually disturb the civil peace of our said colony; but that all and every person and persons may, from time to time, and at all times hereafter, freely and fully have and enjoy his and their own judgments and consciences in matters of religious concernment.

Under all that formal language, the message came clear: the religious conscience was to be forever free. After 1663, Roger Williams often found it necessary to remind his quarreling neighbors that "Our Charter excels all in New England or the world as to the souls of men."

Others, by their acts of imitation, demonstrated their agreement with Williams. Just one year after Rhode Island received its charter, New Jersey (recently won from the Dutch) adopted its charter that echoed not only the sentiments but even the words of Rhode Island's. No person, the New Jersey document declared, would in any way be "molested, punished, disquieted, or called in question" for any difference in religious opinion or [New Jersey's addition] "practice." Of course, the charter of New Jersey, like that of Rhode Island, tried to make clear, as had Williams so valiantly, that liberty did not mean anarchy, did not mean moral chaos, and did not mean that all authority could be defied.

Just one year later, in 1665, Charles II granted a charter to Carolina (at first not divided into North and South) that said, in words quickly becoming familiar, that no person would in any way be "molested, punished, disquieted, or called in question for any differences in opinion or practice in matters of religious concernments." Roger Williams may not have made much headway in Massachusetts or Connecticut, but elsewhere his once-radical ideas were catching on.

Pennsylvania, launched in the early 1680s, did not need to lean heavily upon the precedent of Rhode Island. Its founder, William Penn, had boldly written in 1670 about *The Great Case of Liberty of Conscience.* A Quaker, Penn had known the cruelty of religious persecution personally, as had many of his

fellow Quakers in England and Ireland. When he was given a large grant of land in the New World to start his own colony, he determined that it would, from the beginning, be founded on the principle of religious liberty. No person living "peaceably and quietly under the civil government shall in any case be molested or prejudiced for his or her conscientious persuasion or practice." The "his or her" sounds quite modern, but the Quakers, who emphasized the equality of the sexes, had both male and female preachers from the 17th century on.

Back in England, more light gradually dawned. A few years after the death of Roger Williams and the founding of Pennsylvania in 1681, John Locke, a statesman and philosopher, published his first of three *Letters on Toleration* in 1689.

In 1957, the U.S. Post Office recognized the 300th anniversary of the Flushing Remonstrance, a protest by residents of Long Island against the repressive religious policies of Governor Peter Stuyvesant.

Although he used the word "toleration," which Williams did not care for, Locke revealed in the substance of his letter many major agreements with Roger Williams. "I regard it," Locke wrote, "as necessary above all to distinguish between the business of civil government and that of religion." Oh my, what a remarkable development! Williams, were he still alive, would have only wondered if Massachusetts was paying attention. For Williams, some 50 years earlier, had tried in vain to make exactly that point. The civil magistrate operated in one realm, the churches in another. For this, among other reasons, he had been banished.

The civil magistrate, Locke made clear, must concern himself with civil matters only, never with the salvation of souls. "It does not appear," he observed, "that God ever gave any such authority to one man over another as to compel other men to embrace his religion." Like Williams, Locke agreed that the human conscience could not be and must not be forced. "Confiscate a man's goods, imprison or torture his body: such punishments will be in vain." It could only be a matter of regret that Governor John Endicott had also passed to his grave by the time these words were written.

Locke further explained (and in the 17th century these explanations had to be given again and again) that civil government dealt only with matters of this world, never with matters of the world to come. The church, on the other hand, was a purely voluntary society. No one was born into it, no one could be compelled to attend it or support it, no outside force could legislate for it. Does one need bishops or kings to form a church? No, Locke replied. One needs only what the New Testament church had: "Where two or three are gathered together in my name, there am I in the midst of them" (Matthew 18:20). It is the presence of Christ that makes a church, not the blessings of bishops or the commands of magistrates.

But do not rulers have the right, and even the obligation, to punish the heretic and correct errors in doctrine?

Again, Locke replied in the negative. For one thing, he said, rulers are not that smart, and are not that richly endowed with spiritual wisdom. "Only the Supreme Judge of all men" has that wisdom, and only to Him should be granted "the chastisement of the erroneous." Fire and sword are "never proper instruments for refuting errors or instructing and converting men's minds." Should any doubt the force of this proposition, then Locke said, as Williams so often had, just look at history. Consider what religious persecutions have done to humankind: "what limitless occasions for discords and wars, how powerful a provocation to rapines,

In his famous Letters Concerning Toleration *(published in 1689), the English philosopher and statesman John Locke made the case against religious persecution most persuasively. The "letters" had an enduring influence both in England and America.*

slaughters, and endless hatreds." Where was John Locke back in 1644 when Roger Williams so desperately needed him? Unfortunately for Williams, Locke was only 12 years old at the time.

Locke had enormous influence in America in the 18th century, upon the revolutionary generation and then upon the framers of the U.S. Constitution. So Locke, in echoing and often clarifying the sentiments of Roger Williams, became the chief channel of those once unsettling ideas concerning religious liberty. In England, Locke had justified the Glorious Revolution of 1688 ("glorious" because it was bloodless) that deposed King James II from the throne and replaced him with the joint sovereigns William and Mary. If Locke's words could be used to justify a revolution in England in the 17th century, then why not

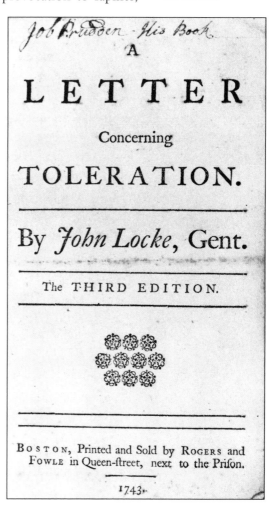

Job Prudden - His Book

A

LETTER

Concerning

TOLERATION.

By *John Locke*, Gent.

The THIRD EDITION.

BOSTON, Printed and Sold by ROGERS and FOWLE in Queen-ftreet, next to the Prifon.

1743.

115

use those words to justify a revolution (not altogether bloodless) in America in the 18th century?

In Virginia, after the American Revolution was won, many argued about how free religion should be. All agreed that the Church of England should no longer be the official, tax-supported, legally protected religion of the state. But just what did the new religious liberty demand? Patrick Henry and others thought that it would be a good idea to make Christianity itself the official religion of Virginia. Toleration, but not yet freedom, in religion. James Madison and others thought Henry's idea was not only a bad one, but beyond that, it betrayed the spirit of what the Revolution was all about. To resist the party and program of Patrick Henry, Madison composed what was called *A Memorial and Remonstrance*—that is, a petition and a protest—to be presented to the Virginia Assembly.

In this document, which was designed to gather as many signatures as possible, Madison assembled a wide variety of arguments to make the case against any official religion. Not the Church of England, not the Presbyterians or Methodists or Catholics, not even Christianity itself—the civil government should simply keep its hands off religion. Sounding very much like Roger Williams, James Madison noted that "torrents of blood have been spilt in the old world, by vain attempts of the secular arm to extinguish religious discord, by proscribing [forbidding] all difference in religious opinion." Madison would have the New World follow a different path. "The American theatre has exhibited proofs that equal and complete liberty" was the best remedy for religious strife and intolerant persecution.

Sounding very much like John Locke, Madison also pointed out that civil magistrates are not all that wise in religious matters. All one need do is look "at the contradictory opinions of rulers in all ages." Furthermore, once the magistrate thinks he is smart enough to rule on matters of doctrine, he begins to think that he is powerful enough to "employ religion as an engine of civil policy." Then we have, said Madison, a political tyranny as bad as the one we just threw off by waging war against England. The American Revolution created a nation prepared to offer a refuge "to the persecuted and oppressed of every nation and religion." This is "the lustre of our country" and nothing should be allowed to dim or destroy it.

Patrick Henry's bill went down in defeat in 1785. The next year, Thomas Jefferson's Bill for Establishing Religious Freedom, long debated and delayed, became law in Virginia. The new law provided, in words that expanded on Rhode Island's 1663 charter, "That no man shall be compelled to frequent [attend] or support any religious worship, place, or ministry whatsoever, nor shall be enforced, restrained, molested, or burdened in his body or goods, nor shall otherwise suffer on account of his religious opinions or beliefs." The team of Madison and Jefferson was a powerful one, to be sure, but they could not have won the necessary votes without the strong support of such evangelical bodies as the Baptists, Methodists, Quakers, Mennonites, and Presbyterians. At a critical moment in the young nation's history, the heirs of Roger Williams joined with the heirs of European rationalism, or Enlightenment, to write religious liberty firmly into the legal structure of Virginia.

The victories in Virginia in 1785 and 1786 preceded by only a short time the gathering of a Constitutional Convention in Philadelphia in the summer of 1787. The delegates to that convention saw their task as one of establishing a civil government. And civil government, as Roger Williams had repeatedly declared, should leave religion alone. So the Constitution did in fact leave religion largely alone. Only once did the Constitution address religion directly, and that was simply to say what government could not do. "No religious test," said Article VI, "shall ever be required as a qualification to any office or public trust under the United States." England at this time still administered a religious test for officeholding, as did many of the new states in the Union. But the federal government would not. Nor would it affirm any faith, recognize any church, or declare any religious loyalties. Citizens of the new nation would, like those in Rhode Island a century and a half earlier, pledge their allegiance, but "in civil things only."

In the process of ratifying the Constitution, many expressed their concern that religious liberty was not explicitly guaranteed. Thomas Jefferson was only one of a large number who insisted that this liberty had to be clearly proclaimed; it could not be simply "understood" that, since the Constitution had claimed no power in this area, religion would certainly be free. So vital, so precious, a freedom had to be declared, without ambiguity and without delay. To win the necessary votes for ratification, James Madison had to promise that, if the Constitution were ratified, the first order of business in the First Congress would be the passage of a Bill of Rights. After much debate and discussion, the

In framing the fundamental structures of the new American nation after the Revolution, no person had a greater impact than James Madison. Moreover, his dedication to religious liberty and the separation of church and state was uncompromising.

first 10 amendments, commonly referred to as America's Bill of Rights, were passed on to the people for ratification. By 1791, the people had approved. The very first phrase of the First Amendment addressed religion: "Congress shall make no law respecting an establishment of religion or prohibiting the free exercise thereof."

No one person is the author of the First Amendment. James Madison proposed wording that in the end was not adopted. Many other representatives and senators joined in the deliberations that lasted throughout the entire summer of 1789. The task was to find the precise wording that would embody the sentiment neatly expressed by Daniel Carroll, senator from Maryland. "The rights of conscience are, in their nature," Carroll declared, "of peculiar delicacy, and will little bear the gentlest touch of governmental hand." The religion clauses of the First Amendment represented a valiant attempt to keep that "gentlest touch" from invading the private souls of women and men.

It would be too much to claim that these 16 words made everything perfectly clear for the next 200 years or more. In fact, the U.S. Supreme Court has spent a great deal of time and thought determining the exact meaning of these words, citing Roger Williams now and then in its opinions. But again, the emphasis was on what a civil government cannot do: it cannot establish a national church (no Church of America to be compared with the Church of England, for example), and it cannot interfere, except in extraordinary circumstances, with the religious liberties— the "free exercise"—of the American people. The First Amendment did not guarantee everything that it might, but from the perspective of Roger Williams the New World had moved mountains between 1635 and 1791.

What that amendment guaranteed immediately, of course, was that some of the uglier aspects of colonial history would not be repeated in the new nation. No more would Quakers be hanged in Boston Common, nor would Jews be expelled from New Amsterdam (New York), or Baptists be whipped, or Catholics fined, or Presbyterians jailed. The heavy hands (as opposed to Carroll's "gentlest touch") of royal governors and civil magistrates would henceforth be restrained, forever forbidden to scar or injure the inner sanctum of the soul.

The long-term effects of the First Amendment proved even more striking. It gave all religious bodies their full freedom: each church was now on an equal footing with all others, now at liberty to evangelize, to recruit, to spread all across the land. Some denominations tested that liberty very cautiously, as one might with his or her toes test the temperature of the ocean. Others, however, took that amendment as their very own charter and—especially on the American frontier—made religious liberty lively and real. Baptists and the newly organized Methodists were particularly successful in their efforts, so much so that these two groups quickly outnumbered the older, more established denominations such as the Congregationalists and the Episcopalians.

Earlier, back in Rhode Island, some Baptists and others decided that the colony of Roger Williams needed to have its own college, because Massachusetts had its school (Harvard) and Connecticut its (Yale). So the College of Rhode Island, later Brown University, was founded in 1764. Like the Constitution, but more than two decades before that document was drafted, Brown's charter provided that "no religious test" would be applied in that academic community. "On the contrary," the charter read, "all the members hereof shall forever enjoy full, free, absolute, and uninterrupted liberty of conscience." Such words could only have warmed the heart of the long-buried Roger Williams. His spirit had not been forgotten. As a 19th-century president of Brown, Francis Wayland, observed in 1860: the Pilgrims and Puritans sought religious liberty for themselves; Roger Williams sought it "for humanity." There are some men, Wayland added, "whose monuments are everywhere."

Thirteen years after the chartering of Brown, a Baptist pastor and historian in Massachusetts, Isaac Backus, published the first volume of his major work, *A History of New England, with Particular Reference to the Denomination of Christians Called Baptists* (1777). In it Backus would, among other things, correct Cotton Mather's 1702 *Ecclesiastical History of New England,* which mentioned Baptists only to dismiss or disparage them. For Mather, Providence Plantations was

an example of an "ungospelized plantation." It contained every imaginable kind of religious dissenter and sectarian noisemaker. Within its borders, said Mather, Rhode Island had "everything in the world but Roman Catholics and real Christians." Backus would also set that record straight.

He would do so, in part, by bringing Roger Williams to the forefront of his history. Backus believed that too many people had forgotten all about Williams and what he had stood for and fought for, even though he had been dead less than a century. Especially in the midst of the American Revolution, it was important to recall what Williams had to say on behalf of liberty—all liberty, civil and religious. Gathering many letters by Williams that might otherwise have been lost, along with other rare documents, Backus reviewed the expulsion of Williams from Boston, the founding of Providence and of its first church, his work with the Indians, the publication of his *Bloudy*

University Hall is the original building of Brown University, founded in 1764. Baptists led in the creation of Brown, and the spirit of Roger Williams is faithfully reflected in its charter, which declared that all students and staff "shall forever enjoy full, free, absolute, and uninterrupted liberty of conscience."

Tenent—and more. Backus concluded that he knew of no other individual in that time period "who acted so consistently and steadily upon right principles about government and liberty as Mr. Williams did."

In an effort to be true to that heritage, Isaac Backus also acted consistently and steadily on behalf of liberty. He had to resist Massachusetts, as Williams had done, though by this time the new state neither banished Baptists nor tied them to whipping posts. It did, however, require Baptists to register and apply for a certificate that would excuse them from paying taxes to support the Congregational Church—still the official and established church of Massachusetts. Backus refused to register and refused to pay the church taxes on the grounds that government was for civil affairs only. In 1774 all Boston was angry over the British tax on tea, Backus pointed out, so much so that the Boston Tea Party resulted in the throwing of many casks of tea into Boston Harbor. Fine, said Backus, but you could avoid the tea tax simply by not drinking tea.

In contrast, he said, you—the leaders of Massachusetts—have placed a tax on our conscience, on our "soul liberty." For you require us either to pay your little tax or you threaten to lay a greater one upon us. But "we are determined not to pay either of them," Backus affirmed, "not only upon your principle of not being taxed where we are not represented, but also because we dare not render that homage to any earthly power which I and many of my brethren are fully convinced belongs only to God." Standing as firm as Williams had boldly stood before the General Court in 1635, Backus concluded: "Here, therefore, we claim charter rights, liberty of conscience."

Backus lived to see his fellow Americans victorious in the Revolution against England, but he did not live long enough to see Massachusetts surrender its grip on religion. Not until 1833 were the last cords cut that tied the church to the state in Massachusetts. Up until that time, the state's constitution called "for the support and maintenance of public Protestant teachers of piety, religion, and morality." Taxes continued to be collected for that purpose, and consciences continued to be insulted by the government's demands in an area that "belongs only to God." Connecticut, similarly wedded to a union of church and state, had achieved separation some- what earlier—in 1818, still nearly three decades after the First Amendment had been drafted. When this Connecticut disestablishment took place, former president Thomas Jefferson in Virginia wrote to ex-president John Adams in Massachusetts expressing his delight that "this den of priest- hood is at length broken up, and that a Protestant popedom is no longer to disgrace American history and character."

Other victories for religious liberty came slowly as well. After the American Revolution, only the New England states (apart from Rhode Island, of course) continued to maintain their official ties with the Congregational Church. But many other states retained language in their constitu- tions that limited officeholding to Protestants or Christians or those who affirmed "that the holy scriptures of the Old and New Testaments are of divine inspiration, and are the rule of faith and practice" (South Carolina, 1778). The 1796 constitution of the state of Tennessee decreed that "no person who denies the being of God, or a future state of rewards and punishments, shall hold any office in the civil department of this State." Not very "civil," Roger Williams might well have observed. One by one the states dropped these various "religious tests," though not until 1961 did the Supreme Court review a religious test (belief in God) as a requirement for officeholding in Maryland. At that time the court declared that neither a state nor the federal gov- ernment could constitutionally force a person "to profess a belief or a disbelief in any religion." Religious liberty could tally up another victory.

On the other hand, many Americans in the 19th century continued to be distressed about these "victories." They saw

FREEDOM: A CONDITION OF THE SPIRIT

Harvard's Perry Miller, the most prominent authority on "the New England mind," also found much to commend in the life and thought of the founder of Rhode Island, who spent great time protesting significant portions of that mind. Miller's book Roger Williams: His Contribution to the American Tradition *(1953) concludes with this evaluation.*

For the subsequent history of what became the United States, Roger Williams possesses one indubitable importance, that he stands at the beginning of it. Just as some great experience in the youth of a person is ever afterward a determinant of his personality, so the American character has inevitably been molded by the fact that in the first years of colonization there arose this prophet of religious liberty. Later generations may not always have understood his thought; they may have imagined that his premises were something other than the actual ones, but they could not forget him or deny him. He exerted little or no direct influence on theorists of the Revolution and the Constitution...yet as a figure and a reputation he was always there to remind Americans that no other conclusion than absolute religious freedom was feasible in this society. The image of him in conflict with the righteous founders of New England could not be obliterated; all later righteous men would be tormented by it until they learned to accept his basic thesis, that virtue gives them no right to impose on others their own definitions. As a symbol, Williams has become an integral element in the meaning of American democracy, along with Jefferson and Lincoln.

However, the student of Williams's own writings will, I trust, perceive that great as has been his symbolic role, he himself was thinking on a deeper plane than that which simply recognizes religious liberty as a way for men to live peaceably together. He was not a rationalist and a utilitarian who gave up the effort to maintain an orthodoxy because he had no real concern about religious truth, but was the most passionately religious of men. Hence he is an analyst, an explorer into the dark places, of the very nature of freedom. His decision to leave denominations free to worship as they chose came as a consequence of his insight that freedom is a condition of the spirit.

them as defeats for the point of view that John Cotton had so vigorously maintained against Roger Williams, and as defeats for the kind of close ties that Massachusetts and Connecticut had maintained between church and state. They also did not approve of the "silences" of the U.S. Constitution with respect to religion.

A National Reform Association, organized in 1864, took as its purpose making the Christian character of national government more explicit. Members of the association thought that the U.S. Constitution should have a clearly religious preamble that would read like this: "Recognizing Almighty God as the source of all authority and power in civil government, and acknowledging the Lord Jesus Christ as the Governor among the nations, His revealed will as the supreme law of the land..." This long clause would be followed by the familiar "We the people" preamble. The association failed, however, to gain enough support for its change to be made. The civil government of the United States would remain civil. And the reputation of Roger Williams would continue to increase.

Even in Massachusetts. There, a native son and Harvard-trained historian, George Bancroft, startled his fellow citizens by offering a dramatically different appraisal of Roger Williams than that of a John Cotton or a Cotton Mather. In the first volume (1834) of what would ultimately become a 12-volume *History of the United States,* Bancroft praised Williams as "the first person in modern Christendom to establish civil government on the doctrine of liberty of conscience, [and] equality of opinion before the law." With respect to Rhode Island, that colony was small in size but large in the "excellency of the principles on which it rested its earliest institutions." Bancroft concluded by calling for the name of Roger Williams to "be preserved in universal history as one who advanced moral and political science, and made himself a benefactor of his race"—the human race.

Bancroft's opinion of Williams may not have been widely shared in the Massachusetts of the 1830s. But a century later, the state of Massachusetts took a remarkable step: it apologized to Roger Williams. The form that this 1936 apology took was a legislative bill that read as follows: "That the sentence of expulsion against Roger Williams by the General Court of Massachusetts Bay Colony in the year sixteen hundred and thirty-five be and hereby is revoked." If Williams had been holding his breath in anticipation of his banishment being erased from history, he would have held that breath for 301 years.

If Massachusetts could be so gracious, no doubt the state of Rhode Island should do something more to honor its founder. So since 1939, atop that steep hill at the bottom of which the first settlers had divided the land and built their homes, a statue of Roger Williams has looked out over

The oldest synagogue in America, Touro Synagogue in Newport, Rhode Island, stands as testimony to the liberty of conscience championed by Roger Williams and by his colony.

his modern city. With considerable fanfare and celebration, the statue was dedicated on a June afternoon with a military band providing the background for a lusty singing of the national anthem. Williams had pleaded for religious liberty for all: Jew, Roman Catholic, Muslim—whomever. It was most appropriate, therefore, that on this occasion the state's Roman Catholic bishop delivered the invocation and the rabbi of Temple Emanu-El offered the benediction. Religious pluralism was not only possible; it could be celebrated, as could the memory of Roger Williams.

The oldest Quaker Yearly Meeting in New England, also in Newport, further illustrates the religious pluralism that Roger Williams helped initiate, a pluralism that would eventually spread throughout America.

At least two other major strides toward "a full liberty in religious concernments" should be noted. For three years, the bishops of the Roman Catholic Church, worldwide, met in Rome in the most significant church council of modern times: Vatican II (1962–65). In the course of the deliberations and the voting on many matters, religious liberty was often mentioned. But disagreements kept postponing a full discussion of the subject until the very end. Then, under the astute, if often despairing, leadership of an American Jesuit, John Courtney Murray, the subject finally held center stage. And the Vatican Council in 1965 passed its "Declaration on Religious Freedom" that moved mountains as dramatically as the First Amendment had.

At this point in human history, the Roman Catholic Church placed itself, officially and firmly, on the side of religious liberty. "This Vatican Synod," the formal document read, "declares that the human person has a right to religious freedom. This freedom means that all men are to be immune from coercion on the part of individuals or of social groups and of any human power." Civil magistrates of the present age, no less than persecuting bishops of an earlier age, must take note. Sometimes called the American document, the "Declaration on Religious Freedom" gave off subtle fragrances of the language of James Madison, Thomas Jefferson, the Rhode Island charter, and Roger Williams.

In 1978, the U.S. Congress passed the Indian Religious Freedom Act, guaranteeing to Native Americans what all other Americans had been granted nearly 200 years before. Why was such an act required in the late 20th century? The answer lay in the many violations of sites, objects, and rituals sacred to the Indian. And so Congress, taking a deep breath, declared "that henceforth it shall be the policy of the United States to protect and preserve for American Indians their inherent right of freedom to believe, express, and exercise the traditional religions of the American Indian, Eskimo, Aleut, and Native Hawaiians, including but not limited to access to sites, use and possession of sacred objects, and the freedom to worship through ceremonial and traditional rites." In 1643, Williams had provided *A Key* to the understanding of the Narraganset and other native tribes. Now, more than 300 years later, Congress had found another key.

Being a small state, Rhode Island through most of its history had had no national park. But in 1984, after long lobbying and patient persuading, the state won its first and only such park: the Roger Williams National Memorial. A small parcel of land, just more than four acres and located within a few dozen yards of where Williams built his first shelter, the National Memorial was designed to keep the memory and legacy of the state's founder alive. In delivering the main address at the dedication of the Memorial, Rhode Island's Senator Claiborne Pell told his audience that in 1636 some 13 families banded together to create "the first genuine democracy—also the first church-divorced and conscience-free community—in modern history." This event in America's history, no less than in Rhode Island's, received commemoration and celebration as bands played and flags flew on that October afternoon.

In 1984 the National Park Service paid tribute to Roger Williams by creating Rhode Island's only national park. Though very small, only four and a half acres, this park (technically a "monument") gave recognition to a large idea: the liberty of conscience.

Roger Williams wrote and spoke a great deal and much of that written and oral record has not survived. Enough has been preserved, however, to fill seven volumes in modern printings. One can distill from those volumes his deep respect for the dignity of every human being, of whatever race, creed, or color. To preserve that dignity, and in particular to protect the spiritual integrity of each person, the essential ingredient is religious liberty. And to preserve the political order, this liberty must be coupled with responsibility. Finally, to maintain any sort of social harmony, Roger Williams also argued for civility. His bequest to America, then, of liberty, responsibility, and civility has enriched the American past and can help to preserve the American future.

CHRONOLOGY

1603
Probable date of Roger Williams's birth in London; King James I succeeds Queen Elizabeth I on the throne of England

1625
King James dies; Charles I becomes king

1627
Williams receives his Bachelor of Arts degree from Pembroke College, Cambridge University

1629
Marries Mary Barnard

1630
Williams and his wife sail for New England

1631
Resides briefly in Boston, then Salem, then Plymouth Colony

1633
Leaves Plymouth Colony to return to Salem for a stormy and controversial two years

1635
In October, the General Court of Massachusetts Bay Colony banishes Williams

1636
Walks from Salem to Narragansett Bay, where he establishes the tiny settlement of Providence

1637
Creates an Indian trading post near the Narraganset tribe

1638
Allocates town lots to first settlers; helps found the first Baptist church in America

1642
Civil war begins in England

1643
Sails from New Amsterdam for London; publishes there *A Key into the Language of America*

1644
Obtains from Parliament a charter for Providence Plantations; publishes *The Bloudy Tenent;* returns to Rhode Island

1649
Charles I is beheaded

1651
Sails with John Clarke for London; holds theological discussions with Oliver Cromwell

1654
After publishing several works in London, returns to Providence, where he is elected president

1657
Retires from public office

1660
In England, the monarchy is restored as Charles II comes to the throne

1663
King Charles II grants royal charter to the colony of Rhode Island and Providence Plantations

1672
For several days, Williams debates with the Quakers, both in Newport and Providence

1676
King Philip's War erupts throughout New England; Williams's own home burns to the ground

1683
Williams dies in the early months of the year

FURTHER READING

THE WRITINGS OF ROGER WILLIAMS

Williams, Roger. *The Bloudy Tenent of Persecution.* Edited by Richard Groves. Macon, Ga.: Mercer University Press, 2001. A readable and accessible edition of Williams's most famous treatise.

————. *Experiments of Spiritual Life and Health.* Edited by Winthrop S. Hudson. Philadelphia: Westminster Press, 1951. This small booklet, written by Williams for the spiritual and physical health of his wife, is expertly introduced and edited.

————. *The Correspondence of Roger Williams.* Edited by Glenn W. LaFantasie. 2 vols. Hanover, N. H.: University Press of New England, 1988. A marvelously thorough and helpful edition of Williams's letters, with extensive notes, useful maps, and an excellent index.

————. *Roger Williams: His Contribution to the American Tradition.* Edited by Perry Miller. Indianapolis: Bobbs-Merrill, 1953. This small anthology did much to rescue the reputation of Roger Williams in modern America, as well as to present limited excerpts of his writings in an attractive form.

————. *A Key into the Language of America.* Edited by John J. Teunissen and Evelyn J. Hinz. Detroit: Wayne State University Press, 1973. This, Williams's first published book, was popular in London in the 17th century and has remained popular in America. This modern edition further enhances that popularity and extends the book's availability.

————. *The Complete Writings of Roger Williams.* 7 vols. New York: Russell & Russell, 1963. Six of these volumes were originally published between 1866 and 1874. The seventh, containing new discoveries and valuable introductions, was added in 1963.

WRITINGS ABOUT WILLIAMS AND HIS CONTEMPORARIES

Gaustad, Edwin S. *Church and State in America.* New York: Oxford University Press, 1999. An illustrated history of the development, and detours, of religious liberty in America.

————. *Liberty of Conscience: Roger Williams in America.* Valley Forge, Pa.: Judson Press, 1999. A thorough biographical treatment of Rhode Island's founder and religious liberty's champion.

Hall, Timothy L. *Separating Church and State: Roger Williams and Religious Liberty.* Urbana: University of Illinois Press, 1998. A professor at the University of Mississippi Law School carefully interprets the legal impact and enduring significance of Roger Williams.

James, Sydney V. *John Clarke and His Legacies: Religion and Law in Colonial Rhode Island.* Edited by Theodore Dwight Bozeman. University Park: Pennsylvania State University Press, 1999. The first full-length treatment of John Clarke written by a skilled historian; gives major attention to the Newport pastor's theology as well as his lasting achievements in politics and philanthropy.

McLoughlin, William G. *New England Dissent: The Baptists and the Separation of Church and State.* 2 vols. Cambridge: Harvard University Press, 1971. Comprehensive in a way that no previous work on this topic had ever been, these two volumes place Roger Williams, John Clarke, Isaac Backus, and others in their proper historical and denominational context.

Miller, William Lee. *The First Liberty: Religion and the American Republic.* New York: Knopf, 1986. Written primarily to celebrate the 200th anniversary of Thomas Jefferson's "Statute for Establishing Religious Freedom in Virginia" (1786), this study gives ample attention to the earlier labors of Roger Williams.

Morgan, Edmund S. *The Puritan Dilemma: The Story of John Winthrop.* Boston: Little, Brown, 1958. This popular biography, as readable as it is reliable, gives Williams's sometime friend and sometime critic the careful examination that he deserves.

————. *Roger Williams: The Church and the State.* New York: Harcourt, Brace, 1967. Yale's Professor Morgan manages to be sympathetic not only to the Puritans but also to their most tenacious critic, Roger Williams.

Noonan, John T., Jr. *The Believer and the Powers That Are*. New York: Macmillan, 1987. One-time dean of the Boalt Law School in Berkeley, California, and now a federal judge, Noonan skillfully reviews the development of religious liberty in the Western world generally and the United States in particular. He also offers generous excerpts of relevant U.S. Supreme Court decisions.

Winslow, Ola E. *Master Roger Williams: A Biography*. New York: Macmillan, 1957. An excellent biography that gives more attention to Williams's London years than does any other book.

Ziff, Larzer, ed. *John Cotton on the Churches of New England*. Cambridge: Harvard University Press, 1968. "The greatest preacher in the first decades of New England history," Cotton was also Roger Williams's greatest antagonist; here he is permitted to speak for himself, without constant interruption.

INDEX

ACKNOWLEDGMENTS

Through the courtesy of Vice President and Editorial Director Nancy Toff of Oxford, I was invited to contribute this study to the Oxford Portraits series for young adults. Somehow, amid countless and growing administrative duties, she found time to give the manuscript an acute and attentive reading.

Beyond that point, Kathryn Hamilton took on the large task of turning a manuscript into a book. With great care she juggled words, illustrations, and deadlines with consummate skill and unfailing grace. She never lost her cool and, more remarkably, never provoked the author into losing his. To both Nancy and Kathryn, my profound thanks.

Many others in the young adult division also assisted in a variety of ways, demonstrating that this business of bringing out a book can actually be pleasant.

PICTURE CREDITS

TEXT CREDITS

p. 24: From *The Correspondence of Roger Williams,* Vol. 1, ed. Glenn W. LaFantasie (Hanover, N.H.: University Press of New England, 1988), 65-9.

p. 41: From *The Complete Writings of Roger Williams,* Vol. 3 (New York: Russell & Russell, 1963), 19-20 (79-80).

p. 80: From *The Correspondence of Roger Williams,* Vol. 2, ed. Glenn W. LaFantasie (Hanover, N.H.: University Press of New England, 1988), 534-40.

p. 89: From *The Complete Writings of Roger Williams,* Vol. 3 (New York: Russell & Russell, 1963), 136-37.

p. 124: From *Roger Williams: His Contribution to the American Tradition,* ed. Perry Miller (Indianapolis: Bobbs-Merrill, 1953), 254-55.

Edwin S. Gaustad is emeritus professor of history at the University of California, Riverside. He is the coauthor, with Philip L. Barlow, of *The New Historical Atlas of Religion in America* (Oxford, 2001), and the author of numerous books on religious history, including *Church and State in America* (Oxford, 1999), *Liberty of Conscience: Roger Williams in America, Neither King nor Prelate: Religion and the New Nation, Sworn on the Altar of God: A Religious Biography of Thomas Jefferson, A Documentary History of Religion in America* (2 vols.), and *A Religious History of America.*